OSPREY COMBAT AIRCRAFT • 50

B-52 STRATOFORTRESS UNITS IN OPERATION *DESERT STORM*

SERIES EDITOR: TONY HOLMES

OSPREY COMBAT AIRCRAFT • 50

B-52 STRATOFORTRESS UNITS IN OPERATION *DESERT STORM*

JON LAKE

OSPREY
PUBLISHING

Front cover

With Operation *Desert Storm* just a matter of hours old, 12 B-52Gs launched from Wurtsmith AFB, Michigan, into the early morning darkness on 18 January 1991. Bound for targets deep inside Iraq, these aircraft had just commenced what would become the longest employ-deploy strike mission in history, up to this time. The aircraft consisted of seven 'Buffs' from the 379th BW, three from the 93rd and two from the 42nd, split into three cells of four. And although the aircraft were drawn from a number of units, all were flown by crews from the 524th BS/379th BW. Between them, the dozen jets were carrying a deadly load of 288 CBU-87 cluster bombs and 135 M117 general purpose bombs. The formation consisted of three cells of four B-52s, with a 'spare' aircraft in each cell. Enduring poor weather, unreliable communication with controlling AWACS and jumpy air defence controllers in Egypt, only the four B-52s in Cell 3 dropped bombs in Iraq. Cell 1 was recalled by an E-3 Sentry AWACS, while Cell 2 ran low on fuel when it was forced to bypass a storm.

This artwork by Mark Postlethwaite shows one of the Wurtsmith aircraft from Cell 3 braving intense AAA and SAMs as it presses home its attack on an Iraqi airfield. All four jets emerged from their bombing runs unscathed, and duly landed at King Abdul Aziz International Airport, also known as Jeddah New, in Saudi Arabia, where they joined the 1708th BW(P) (*Cover artwork by Mark Postlethwaite*)

First published in Great Britain in 2004 by Osprey Publishing
1st Floor, Elms Court, Chapel Way, Botley, Oxford, OX2 9LP

ISBN 1 84176 751 4

Edited by Tony Holmes
Page design by Tony Truscott
Cover Artwork by Mark Postlethwaite
Aircraft Profiles and Line Artwork by Mark Styling
Index by Alison Worthington
Origination by Grasmere Digital Imaging, Leeds, UK
Printed in Hong Kong through Bookbuilders

04 05 06 07 08   10 9 8 7 6 5 4 3 2 1

EDITOR'S NOTE
To make this best-selling series as authoritative as possible, the Editor would be interested in hearing from any individual who may have relevant photographs, documentation or first-hand experiences relating to the world's elite pilots, and their aircraft, of the various theatres of war. Any material used will be credited to its original source. Please write to Tony Holmes via e-mail at:
tony.holmes@osprey-jets.freeserve.co.uk

ACKNOWLEDGMENTS
The author would like to thank Maj Andy Bloom (formerly of the 1708th BW(P)), Tony Cassanova, Capt Jim Clonts (formerly of the 1500th SW(P) and the 4300th BW(P)), Jerry Fugere, Maj Blaise Martinick (formerly of the 2nd BW and the 801st BW(P)), Maj Scott Moore (formerly of the 1708th BW(P)), and Capt John Ritter (formerly of the 4300th BW(P)) for their help and advice. Any errors were made in spite of their assistance.

CONTENTS

BACK TO WAR

When Coalition forces went to war against Iraq in January 1991, they did so with the most impressive and capable armada of military aircraft the world had ever seen. This force included the latest F-117 Stealth fighters, F-15E Strike Eagles, E-8 J-STARS, British Tornados and a number of similarly high-tech 'debutantes'. But operating alongside these state-of-the-art aircraft were a number of 'old soldiers', several of which had received their baptisms of fire 26 years before in Vietnam. Not least of these stalwarts were Strategic Air Command's B-52G Stratofortresses, many of which had actually participated in Operations *Arc Light* and *Linebacker*, facing the storm of fire over Hanoi and other North Vietnamese targets (see *Osprey Combat Aircraft 43 – B-52 Stratofortress Units in Combat 1955-73* for details).

Despite its age, the B-52G made a major contribution to the *Desert Storm* air campaign. With an 'official' total of 74 aircraft deployed (64 Primary Aircraft Authorised, plus ten for attrition or as maintenance reserves), the B-52G accounted for 3.5 per cent of the Coalition's 1875 'shooters'. This figure probably represented the peak strength, with some rotation of aircraft meaning that the overall number of B-52Gs committed to the conflict was probably somewhere between 74 and 86. Other official sources put the number of B-52Gs deployed at 66 or 68 aircraft out of a total USAF force of 118 G-models then on strength (representing 58 per cent of the available inventory). The aircraft were accompanied by 155 crews.

Whatever the exact total, only the A-6 Intruder, A-10 Thunderbolt and F-16 Fighting Falcon deployed in larger numbers.

These B-52s flew approximately 1620 sorties (or 1617, 1624, 1706 or 1741, according to various sources), representing just over three per cent of the total air combat missions. In doing so, the ageing 'Buffs' accounted for 30 per cent (or 29 or 34 per cent according to other sources) of the total US bomb tonnage released, thanks to the aircraft's uniquely large payload. This total represented some 72,289 weapons (mainly M117 750-lb bombs, Mk 82 500-lb bombs and CBU-87 and CBU-89 cluster

Its weapons gone, a B-52G in the latest monochromatic grey colour scheme approaches the tanker for a much needed top-up en route back to Diego Garcia. The aircraft's refuelling receptacle doors are already open as the pilot manoeuvres into position (*Andy Bloom*)

bomb units) weighing 25,700,000 lbs (with 11,742,000 lbs of explosives). This was 38 per cent of the USAF bomb tonnage (42 per cent according to some sources). In doing so, the B-52Gs absorbed 3.5 per cent of the tanker effort sortied to support tactical aircraft.

An official post-war USAF study stated that 'The primary role assigned to both B-52G bombers and tactical aircraft was to help prepare the battlefield for an eventual ground assault. The objective of the B-52G's role was psychological. It was to undermine the morale of Iraqi ground forces through periodic bombardment.'

Over two-thirds of the B-52 missions (perhaps as many as 85 per cent) were directed against Iraqi ground forces, leading to the understandable, but inaccurate, public perception that the aircraft did little more than carpet bomb Iraqi armoured units in the open desert. However, the remaining one-third of B-52 sorties were against pinpoint targets, including low-level strikes on enemy airfields (until Night Three), and attacks against military/industrial facilities, electrical power plants and other targets.

Although it was not acknowledged at the time, B-52s operating from the Continental United States (CONUS) even fired some of the opening shots of the campaign, launching a barrage of top-secret Conventionally Air Launched Cruise Missiles (CALCM) against a variety of 'Night One' targets. There was even a contingency plan for the B-52Gs to act as 'tank plinkers', dropping GBU-10 or GBU-12 Paveway laser-guided bombs which would have been designated and 'guided' by Pave Tack-equipped F-111Fs. In the end, the F-111Fs and other tactical types were able to achieve the Central Command (CENTCOM) objective of eliminating half of Iraq's armour and artillery before the ground war began, and the B-52s were not needed as LGB-droppers.

As America and its allies prepared a response to Saddam Hussein's invasion of Kuwait, a force of B-52Gs was assembled for conventional bombing operations. The immediate need was to be able to react if the Iraqis followed up their invasion of Kuwait with a push against Saudi Arabia's oilfields. Initially, US forces were deployed to deter an Iraqi attack on Saudi Arabia. There were some fears that basing a wing-sized force of B-52s in Saudi Arabia would have been provocative, and might risk rapid escalation, so the USAF deployed overtly defensive aircraft

B-52Gs operated in three aircraft 'cells' during *Desert Storm*, just as they had done over Vietnam 20 years before. This gave the best electronic countermeasures 'cross protection' for all three bombers (*Andy Bloom*)

(mainly fighters) to Saudi bases, and looked for a bomber base close enough to allow the aircraft to hit targets in Iraq, but far enough away not to push Saddam into action before the USA was ready.

Almost immediately, planning began for an offensive air campaign aimed at both forcing an Iraqi withdrawal from Kuwait and the 'accomplishment of other national policy objectives. It was intended to destroy Iraq's capability to produce and employ weapons of mass destruction, to destroy Iraq's offensive military capability, to cause the withdrawal of Iraqi forces from Kuwait and to restore the legitimate government of Kuwait.'

The operation would require the coalition to 'gain and maintain air superiority, sever Iraqi supply lines, destroy chemical, biological and nuclear capability, and destroy Republican Guard forces'.

The order detailed three centres of gravity to be targeted for destruction throughout the offensive campaign. These were Iraq's national command authority, its nuclear-biological-chemical capability and the Republican Guard forces.

During Operation *Desert Shield*, which lasted from early August 1990 through to 16 January 1991, US and Coalition planners drew up a series of increasingly refined and progressively more ambitious offensive plans while deploying massive forces to the region. *Desert Shield* also gave US planners time to study, locate and identify important strategic targets in Iraq, and to accumulate intelligence on the nature of Iraqi air defences.

During the six months of *Desert Shield* the Coalition was able to deploy all the required forces, using largely existing infrastructure on foreign, yet friendly, soil that directly bordered the theatre of war, while the enemy did little to obstruct the process. The deployed units were also given sufficient time to practise flying in the desert environment, honing their skills under conditions for which most had not previously trained, given the previous expectation that large-scale combat would take place in a European scenario.

The operational order issued by the commander in chief of CENTCOM on the eve of the offensive campaign launched 'a four-phase air, naval and ground offensive operation'. The first three phases essentially comprised the air campaign, and the last phase covered the ground offensive.

The Central Air Force Director of Air Campaign Plans estimated that the ground offensive would require 18 days, with the total campaign taking 32 days, and there were some hopes that the ground offensive would actually be rendered unnecessary by the effectiveness of the Coalition air offensive. This in turn was deliberately progressive and proportional, so that the first phase of the offensive was concentrated against leadership-related targets deep inside Iraq, hoping to force Saddam Hussein to withdraw from Kuwait even before the Coalition could unleash the full force of its military machine. If the destruction of key leadership facilities ranging from the presidential palaces to critical communications nodes did not result in an Iraqi collapse, then the USAF planned to destroy elite Republican Guard units in the Kuwait Theatre of Operations (KTO), which were a key prop to Saddam's regime.

CENTCOM's operational orders now called for an 'effects-based' plan to be formulated, with one of its aims being the shutting down of the national electricity power grid, thus preventing the Iraqi leadership from transmitting orders and receiving information from troops in the field. It did not specify the precise level of damage to be inflicted on individual targets or target sets, and indeed sought to avoid unnecessary destruction. Thus the campaign was precisely targeted to destroy critical nodes, such as the generating halls of electric power plants or the telephone switching centres in Baghdad.

In order to attack these targets, the Coalition air forces first had to attack Iraq's strategic air defences and the country's strategic chemical, biological and nuclear weapons capability. The list of strategic targets to be attacked during the first two or three days of 'Phase I' grew from 84 in late August 1990 to 476 by the eve of the war.

It was estimated that the first phase – the strategic air campaign – would require six to nine days to achieve its objectives.

The second phase of the air campaign was expected to achieve air supremacy throughout the KTO, and was scheduled to last two to four days. Beginning sometime between Day Seven and Day Ten of the campaign, it would end no later than Day 13. Air supremacy was to be achieved by 'attacking aircraft/airfields, air defence weapons and command and control systems in order to roll back enemy air defences'.

The third Phase of 'battlefield preparation' was expected to start between Days Nine and 14, and require eight days to complete. The aim was to reduce Iraqi combat effectiveness in the KTO by at least 50 per cent, and to 'open the window of opportunity for initiating ground offensive operations by confusing and terrorising Iraqi forces in the KTO, and shifting combat force ratios in favour of friendly forces'.

Although the B-52 was expected to play a part in all phases of the air campaign, planners identified that it would be particularly effective in strikes against Iraqi military targets in southern Iraq and Kuwait, 'attacking Iraqi ground combat forces (particularly Republican Guard units) and supporting missile/rocket/artillery units, interdicting supply lines and destroying command, control and communications', in conjunction with tactical aircraft and naval bombardment.

For *Desert Storm*, the USAF deployed its new F-15Es and a sizeable force of F-111Fs, but was unable to send the newest of its heavier bombers, the B-1B and B-52H, which were ill prepared for conventional operations. This left only the ageing B-52Gs available for operations.

Integrated Conventional Stores Management System (ICSMS) equipped B-52Gs then remained in use only with the 2nd BW's 62nd BS at Barksdale AFB and the 42nd BW's 69th BS at Loring AFB. The other 'conventional' units – the 320th BW's 441st BS at Mather

Light shrapnel damaged the port underwing fuel tank of Jeddah-based B-52G 58-0253. A number of 'Buffs' were hit by Iraqi AAA during the conflict, but none were lost to enemy action (*Andy Bloom*)

AFB and the 43rd BW's 60th BS at Andersen AFB, on Guam, had inactivated in September 1989 and April 1990, respectively.

Although operating cruise missile-equipped B-52Gs, and despite being primarily tasked with alert duties using the AGM-86, the remaining units retained a secondary conventional role, and were brought to readiness for deployment alongside the conventional bombers. These units included the Barksdale-based 2nd BW's 596th BS, the 97th BW's 340th BS at Blytheville AFB, the 379th BW's 524th BS at Wurtsmith AFB and the 416th BW's 668th BS at Griffiss AFB. The 93rd BW's 328th BTS at Castle AFB used examples of both B-52G sub-types for training.

The inclusion of these Single Integrated Operational Plan (SIOP) assigned, ALCM-equipped B-52Gs and their crews was to be of crucial importance, since they brought capabilities and skills which the conventional wings did not have – operating at high altitude and in integrated three-aircraft cells. The 'conventional' B-52s, meanwhile, were all equipped with Global Positioning System (GPS), and were thus inevitably used to lead cells.

The first element of seven B-52G bombers assembled for Operation *Desert Storm* were drawn from Loring's 42nd BW, and these deployed on 12 August 1990 carrying full loads of M117R iron bombs, cannon ammunition and chaff and flares so that they could be turned around quickly after their arrival in-theatre.

Over the next three days, further aircraft deployed from one squadron (the 62nd BS) of the 2nd BW, together with a handful of aircraft and crews from the 93rd BW at Castle and from the Griffiss-based 416th BW. These were assigned to the 4300th BW(Provisional), which was hastily formed at Diego Garcia, a British dependency in the Chagos Archipelago, British Indian Ocean Territory, seven degrees south of the Equator, 1000 miles south of India. By 16 August the 4300th was fully formed, with 20 fully armed B-52Gs on alert.

Initially, the B-52s were expected to counter any Iraqi invasion of Saudi Arabia, planning to operate at low altitude, seeking out and bombing enemy forces before egressing over the Persian Gulf. After three weeks,

Three 42nd BW B-52Gs, newly arrived for the 1708th BW(P), share Jeddah's ramp with C-130H Hercules transport aircraft of the Royal Saudi Air Force's No 4 Sqn, while USAF KC-135 tankers are visible in the background (*Andy Bloom*)

Right
Laden with bombs, B-52G 58-0237 takes off from RAF Fairford on one of its nine *Desert Storm* missions (totalling 137.7 hours). The aircraft lost its *Daffy's Destruction* nickname and nose art and even its 379th BW 'Triangle K' tail markings once committed to the conflict (*Duncan Adams/Stewart Lewis and Andy Bloom*)

With its capacious bomb-bay crammed full of bombs, and with two underwing pylons also loaded up, the ageing 'Buff' could carry a formidable load of ordnance to the target. Here, a 1708th BW(P) aircraft takes off for a mission against the Republican Guard (*Andy Bloom*)

this duty passed to A-10 and F-16 units, and B-52 planning turned to fixed targets in Gen Chuck Horner's Air Tasking Order (ATO).

A little known second Stratofortress detachment formed on the island of Guam when six 2nd BW B-52G crews deployed to Andersen AFB on 5 January 1991. Andersen had been arguably the most important B-52 base during the Vietnam War, and had accommodated a B-52 unit of its own (the 43rd BW's 60th BS(Heavy), until it was inactivated on 30 April 1990. Andersen had transferred from the control of Strategic Air Command to the Pacific Air Forces' Thirteenth Air Force in October

1989, but remained a regular destination for B-52 deployments.

From August 1990, Andersen AFB was used as a major staging post for munitions and supplies for US forces in the Persian Gulf, handling more than 37,000 tons. Six crews from 2nd BW deployed to Guam on 5 January 1991, forming the 1500th BW(P). The six jets flew training missions against a nearby island, and the crews also used the simulator left behind by the disbanded 43rd BW.

Another B-52G group, the 1708th BW(P), was formed at

Jeddah's King Abdul Aziz International Airport (Jeddah New) in the week immediately prior to the outbreak of war. Although the base was surveyed as a B-52 Forward Operating Location (FOL) between 16and26 October 1990, and approved for use two days later, the Saudi government only agreed to the deployment of a full B-52 wing to Jeddah two weeks prior to *Desert Storm* commencing. A single B-52G flew in from Diego Garcia for one day of taxiing and parking tests on 20 December, and crews began to deploy in early January.

Jeddah's first six B-52s arrived on the first night of the war from Diego Garcia, with ten more (five from the 379th, three from the 93rd and two from the 42nd) flying in on 18 January after conducting a mission from Wurtsmith. The Diego Garcia B-52s, and four of the Wurtsmith aircraft, flew into Jeddah after first attacking targets in Iraq.

The Diego Garcia-based B-52s which transferred to Jeddah were replaced by the 1500th BW aircraft from Guam, but efforts were soon underway to create an even larger force of B-52s. The 17th Air Division (Provisional) would go on to gain two further provisional bomb wings, although these would be smaller units with fewer aircraft.

Schwarzkopf and his air commander, Gen Horner, had wanted one more B-52 wing located closer to the action, and favoured using Cairo West as its base. Egyptian objections forced a change of plan, however, and two smaller provisional wings were established further away at USAFE bases in England and Spain instead. These joined the action soon after the war had begun.

B-52G 58-0193 *IRON MAIDEN* is something of an enigma. Missing from official lists of participating Stratofortresses, this aircraft was, nevertheless, photographed (above) returning home to the US via RAF Fairford post-war. Its bomb-log seems to indicate that the aircraft flew 13 sorties (probably from Moron), and landed at Jeddah – hence the camel silhouette – on at least one occasion (*Duncan Adams/ Stewart Lewis and David K Donald*)

THE G-MODEL

Operation *Desert Storm* was very much a final curtain for the B-52G, which was given a brief extra lease on life as a direct result of Saddam Hussein's invasion of Kuwait.

The USAF had actually already started to phase the B-52G out of service during 1989, with aircraft being sent to the Aerospace Maintenance and Regeneration Center 'boneyard' at Davis-Monthan AFB in the Arizona desert, where they were to be guillotined into five sections to satisfy the terms of the Reduction and Limitation of Strategic Offensive Arms START treaty.

The B-52G had been the most numerous Stratofortress sub-variant, with 193 being built exclusively at the Wichita factory between October 1958 and February 1961. It had been designed 'from scratch' as a strategic missile carrier, although some began to assume a conventional attack mission when fatigue and attrition took its toll on the conventionally assigned B-52Ds, gaining the same Phase V *Rivet Rambler* electronic warfare upgrades as the B-52D fleet. But following the end of the Vietnam War, the G-model returned to nuclear duties, augmenting the later B-52H.

Throughout the 1970s, the B-52G/H formed the backbone of the USAF's strategic nuclear deterrent, while the B-52D continued primarily in the tactical and conventional roles. A total of 270 B-52G/Hs were modified to carry the Boeing AGM-69A Short Range Attack Missile (SRAM) from 1971. SRAM was a stand-off nuclear missile with a solid fuel rocket engine giving a maximum range of about 100 miles. Eight were carried on a rotary launcher in the bomb-bay, and 12 more could be hung in triples on the underwing pylons. SRAM gradually replaced the Hound Dog, which was finally phased out completely in 1978. SRAM

57-6468 was the first production B-52G, and thus the first production 'Buff' with the shorter, square cut tail fin, although this had initially been tested on an early B-52A. The aircraft also introduced a new lightweight wing (*Author's collection*)

The B-52G's early career was spent as part of SAC's nuclear deterrent. This Hound Dog missile-armed G-model (58-0159) fought during *Desert Storm* as *Alley Oops Bold Assault*, deploying from the 379th BW to fly operations from Jeddah and Fairford (*Author's collection*)

Another Fairford-based *Desert Storm* warrior was 58-0182, seen here earlier in its life during refuelling trials with the proposed KC-747, which dwarfed the USAF's heavy bomber (*Author's collection*)

itself remained in service until 1990, when it was phased out due to concerns about warhead reliability.

The demands of the nuclear mission placed an ever greater emphasis on low-level and all-weather penetration, as well as on countering ever more sophisticated enemy defences. This led to major modifications to the B-52, which transformed the airframes which had battled it out over Vietnam into what virtually amounted to a new bomber.

58-0237 also flew *Desert Storm* missions from Fairford, although it is seen here during an earlier incarnation as a Skybolt missile trials aircraft (*Author's collection*)

The ambitious *Rivet Ace* Phase VI ECM Defensive Avionics Systems (ECP2519) upgrade was launched in December 1971, and as the development became protracted, the overall price for the project escalated from $362.5 million to $1.5 billion. It took several years to fit the upgrades into every B-52G.

The *Rivet Ace* testbed (58-0204) trialled a variety of ECM systems and flew with a number of different antenna configurations. Unlike production Phase VI aircraft, the prototype carried its ALQ-153 tail warning radar in a pod mounted on the tip of the port stabilator instead of inside the fin, covered by deep blisters on each side. With ALQ-172 (later adopted as the Phase VI+ fit), the aircraft had unusual antennae below the rudder and 'cheek fairings' further aft and higher up – close to the cockpit side windows. However, on the 'production' Phase VI+ conversions, the equipment re-used the standard ALQ-117 fairings.

Threat warning systems used in the definitive Phase VI EW suite included an AN/ALR-20A countermeasures receiver, an AN/ALR-46(V) digital radar warning receiver set and an AN/ALQ-153 tail warning radar

58-0204 served as the *Rivet Ace* ECM testbed, with its ALQ-153 ECM equipment being housed in a unique tailplane-mounted fairing. This aircraft had previously fought in Operation *Linebacker*, and went on to fly operational missions during *Desert Storm* as *Special Delivery* of the 379th BW, flying from Fairford as part of the 806th BW(P) (*Author's collection*)

The silver and anti-flash white 'Chrome Dome' colour scheme gave way to SIOP camouflage, with three-tone camouflage top surfaces and a white nose. Soon afterwards, the 'Buffs' received a 'nose job' with the addition of undernose EVS turrets and new EW antennae (*Author's collection*)

set. The Phase VI upgrade also added an AN/ALQ-117 active countermeasures set, with a pair of antennae inside teardrop-shaped cheek fairings on each side of the nose above the Electro-optical Viewing System (EVS) turrets, and with further antennae in the extended tail cone, which was stretched by 40 inches to house extra electronic equipment.

Phase VI also added the AN/ALQ-122 false target generator system (sometimes known as Smart Noise Operation Equipment), AN/ALT-28 noise jammers (with a prominent antenna fairing projecting upwards from the top of the nose radome), AN/ALT-32H and AN/ALT-32L high-and low-band jamming sets and an AN/ALT-16A barrage-jamming system.

The upgraded B-52Gs also carried a much expanded array of expendables, with 12 AN/ALE-20 flare dispensers (containing a total of 192 flares) and eight AN/ALE-24 chaff dispensers (with 1125 chaff bundles). The latter were housed in the wing trailing edge, just outboard of the inner engine pod in the vacant space between the two sets of flaps.

Some aircraft had the new EW equipment fitted at the same time that they gained the AN/ASQ-151 EVS, or immediately afterwards, and it was very unusual to see aircraft fitted with EVS alone. The EVS sytstem was fitted to all surviving B-52Gs and B-52Hs between 1972 and 1976, and was designed to give crews an enhanced view of the outside world when flying at low level at night. The system consisted of two separate sensors contained in two fairings below the nose. When not in use, the EVS sensors could be rotated to face aft 'into the fairings' for protection against damage from FOD. The sensor windows included built-in 'washers'.

A Hughes AN/AAQ-6 forward-looking infrared (FLIR) sensor was housed in the starboard fairing, with a steerable Westinghouse AN/AVQ-22 low-light-level television camera to port. New CRT display screens were installed at the pilot, co-pilot and both navigator stations. A variety of information could be overlaid on the TV or FLIR picture, including alphanumerics indicating sensor position (invaluable if the sensor was not boresighted), indicated airspeed, time-to-weapons release, a radar altimeter height readout and heading error. The screens could also be used to display an artificial horizon overlay or a graphic of the terrain avoidance profile trace.

With the abandonment of airborne alert, and with improving enemy weapons, greater emphasis was placed on rapid reaction take-offs by the USAF's nuclear-armed bombers. As part of the $35 million Project *Quick Start*, launched in 1974, cartridge starters were fitted to all unmodified B-52G/H engines (each aircraft had already had such starters fitted to two engines since 1963-64).

In the early 1980s, 98 of 166 surviving B-52Gs were also converted to carry the AGM-86 Air-Launched Cruise Missile (ALCM), sharing the weapon with all 96 remaining H-models. ALCM-capable jets became operational with the 416th BW at Griffiss in December 1982.

From 1980, 168 B-52Gs and 96 B-52Hs, including all of the cruise missile carriers, received a new digital AN/ASQ-176 Offensive Avionics System (OAS), which allowed them to fully exploit the new weapon. The new OAS included dual AN/ASN-136 inertial navigation systems, AN/APN-218 Doppler, an AN/ASN-134 attitude heading reference system and an AN/APN-224 radar altimeter. Major modifications were also made to the primary attack radar, and new digital missile interface units were provided. The system was optimised for low-level use, and was hardened against EMP (electromagnetic pulse). A B-52G flew with the new system on 3 September 1980, and quickly demonstrated much improved reliability.

While half of the B-52G force adopted a cruise missile role, the remainder were assigned to the low level conventional attack mission. Here, a B-52G lets fly with a stick of retarded 500-lb 'Snakeyes' (*Author's collection*)

Having done its duty as the *Rivet Ace* testbed, 58-0204 was then used to test the 'satellite conspicuous' wingroot fairings designed to distinguish those B-52Gs modified to fire ALCMs. The fairings provided a distinctive 'curved' leading edge/root plan view (*Author's collection*)

Under the provisions of the unratified Strategic Arms Limitation Treaty (SALT) II treaty, cruise missile-carrying aircraft had to be readily identifiable as such by orbiting reconnaissance satellites. The B-52Hs, with their turbofan engines, were considered to be sufficiently distinctive, but a means had to be found to differentiate between cruise- and non-cruise-equipped B-52Gs. The chosen solution was to add a distinctive, rounded, non-functional wing root fairing ('strakelet'), to the AGM-86B-equipped jets. The modification had to be structurally integral with the aircraft so that the change could not be easily removed, or moved from one aircraft to another.

Although the USAF stringently adhered to this provision of the SALT II treaty, it broke the strict 130-cruise missile carrier limit, receiving its 131st ALCM-capable Stratofortress (B-52H 60-0055, appropriately nicknamed *Salt Shaker*), on 28 November 1986, and eventually receiving a total of 194 such aircraft – 64 more than it was 'entitled' to.

From 1985, a number of B-52Gs also received the same Norden AN/APQ-156 Strategic Radar that was simultaneously fitted to all surviving B-52Hs, this system replacing the original ASQ-176. The $700 million programme greatly enhanced the B-52's autonomous targeting capability, and included the provision of new controls, displays and software.

Those B-52Gs retained in the conventional role when the bulk of the fleet were converted to carry cruise missiles were equipped with an Integrated Conventional Stores Management System (ICSMS) and fitted with a shorter 'stub' pylon than that employed by ALCM carriers. This pylon was compatible with the original I-beam used on the B-52D, and on other versions using converted Hound Dog pylons, and with a new Heavy Stores Adapter Beam (HSAB) optimised for large and heavy weapons.

When used to carry smaller weapons like the M117 and Mk 82, the I-beam had a larger capacity than the HSAB, carrying 12 bombs each, rather than eight. The HSAB permitted heavier weapons to be carried, however, including five 2000-lb Mk 84 bombs on each pylon, or six AGM-84 Harpoon anti-ship missiles.

By the time of *Desert Storm*, the conventional 'Buffs' were known as Mod 777s, as Navigator Jim Clonts explained:

'The "Triple 7" mods were not cruise missile capable, so they did not have the wing fillets like other CM-modified B-52Gs. The "Triple 7" birds all had Heavy Store Adapter Beams which allowed us to carry up to 2000-lb weapons externally, and they had GPS integrated into the INS/OAS, Digital Bomb Release Interval Control, and KY-58 Secure

Voice. They also had advanced data buses to talk to "smart weapons" on the external pylons.'

Some 30 of the ICSMS B-52Gs were fitted with a Harpoon Aircraft Command Launch Control Set (HACLCS) at the navigator's station, allowing them to carry up to 12 AGM-84 missiles on the underwing HSABs. The 320th BW's 441st BS at Mather acted as the test and evaluation wing for the Harpoon. AGM-84-armed B-52Gs were also delivered to the 42nd BMW's 69th BMS at Loring in 1984, and then to the 43rd BW at

Andersen. All surviving ICSMS-modified B-52Gs were eventually fitted with the HACLCS.

Eight of the ICSMS aircraft were also equipped to carry the AGM-142 Have Nap, a derivative of the Rafael Popeye precision-guided air-to-surface missile jointly developed by Israel's Rafael and Lockheed Martin under the Have Nap programme.

The B-52Gs remaining in service by the late 1980s were thus very different aircraft to those that had seen action in the final stages of the Vietnam War, even though they were often the same basic airframes, bearing the same serial numbers.

At one time it had been intended that the B-52G would serve in the conventional role, while the entire fleet of H-models remained exclusively committed to the stand-off nuclear role using cruise missiles. When force reductions led to the need to slim-down the B-52 inventory, the decision was taken to retire the B-52G, with the B-52H force then adopting the conventional role which it would undertake alongside its nuclear responsibilities.

The main reason for this decision lay in the G-model's water-injected J57 powerplant. Water injection was by then an idea whose time had gone, imposing maintenance and support difficulties, and threatening handling problems if anything went wrong, as one B-52 pilot explained to the author:

'The idea of dumping tons of water into a fire is as absurd as it sounds. If the pumps don't work, or you lose the water augmentation, conditions can become critical. What can also happen is that you can put out the fire in the engine. If you put out two engines in the outboards, you not only lose the engines, but you give yourself a nightmare of a directional control problem. It's a problem that is serious. It gets your attention.'

Ironically, the TF33 turbofans used on the B-52H were almost as old and archaic as the G-model's J57 turbojets, prompting renewed studies into the feasibility of a B-52 re-engining programme during the mid-1990s.

Although *Desert Storm* had interrupted the planned drawdown and realignment of the force, all B-52Gs would be withdrawn from service by the end of 1994.

The bear and sunray badge just visible on the tail fin of 58-2573 identifies it as belonging to the 320th BW at Mather. It is seen here dropping mines during a 1987 exercise. By 1990, the aircraft was flying with the 42nd BW, and it saw action during *Desert Storm* with the 4300th BW(P) (*Author's collection*)

COLOUR PLATES

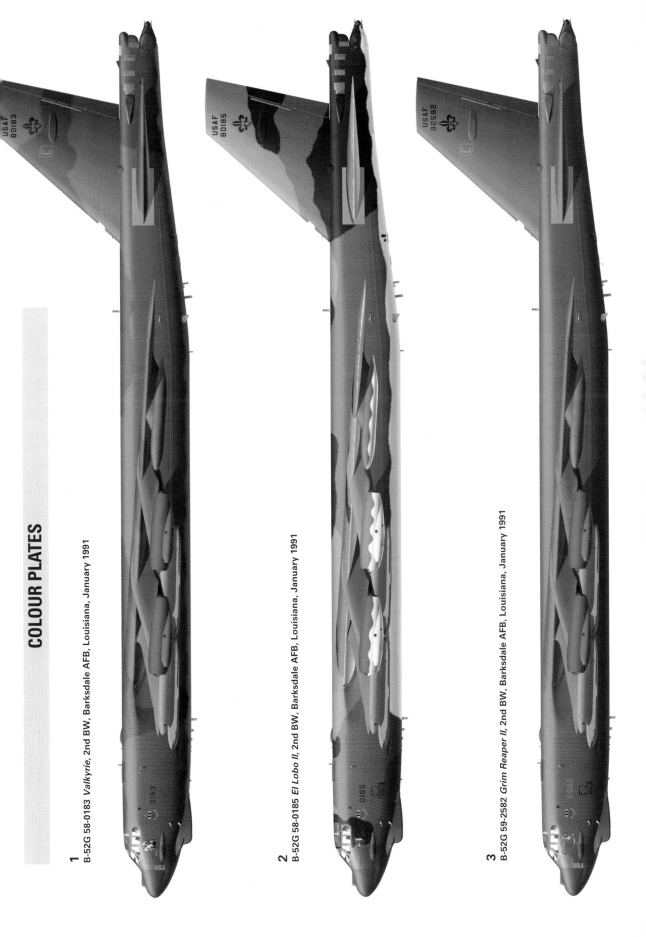

1
B-52G 58-0183 *Valkyrie*, 2nd BW, Barksdale AFB, Louisiana, January 1991

2
B-52G 58-0185 *El Lobo II*, 2nd BW, Barksdale AFB, Louisiana, January 1991

3
B-52G 59-2582 *Grim Reaper II*, 2nd BW, Barksdale AFB, Louisiana, January 1991

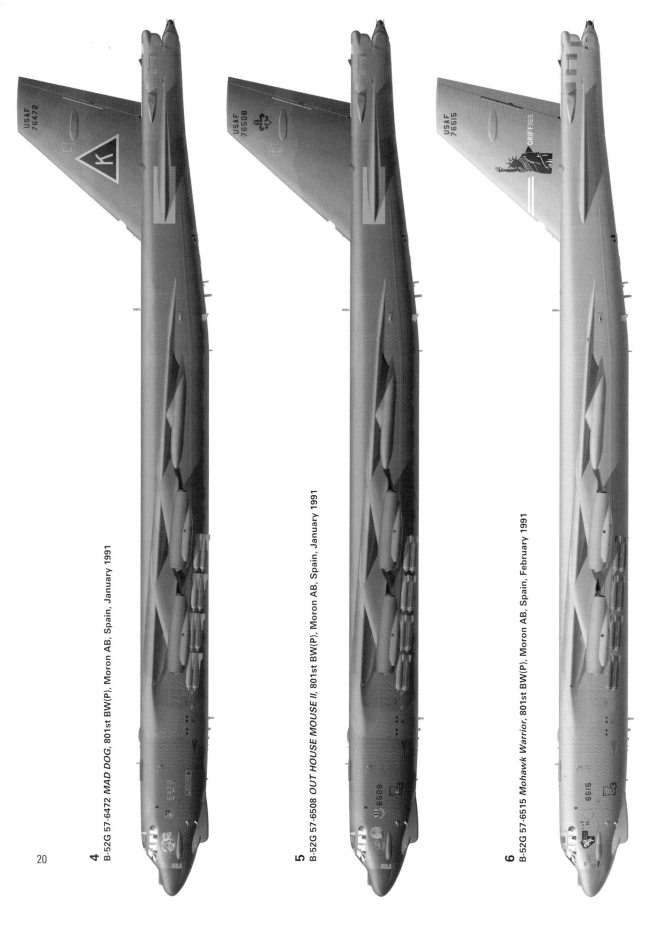

4
B-52G 57-6472 *MAD DOG*, 801st BW(P), Moron AB, Spain, January 1991

5
B-52G 57-6508 *OUT HOUSE MOUSE II*, 801st BW(P), Moron AB, Spain, January 1991

6
B-52G 57-6515 *Mohawk Warrior*, 801st BW(P), Moron AB, Spain, February 1991

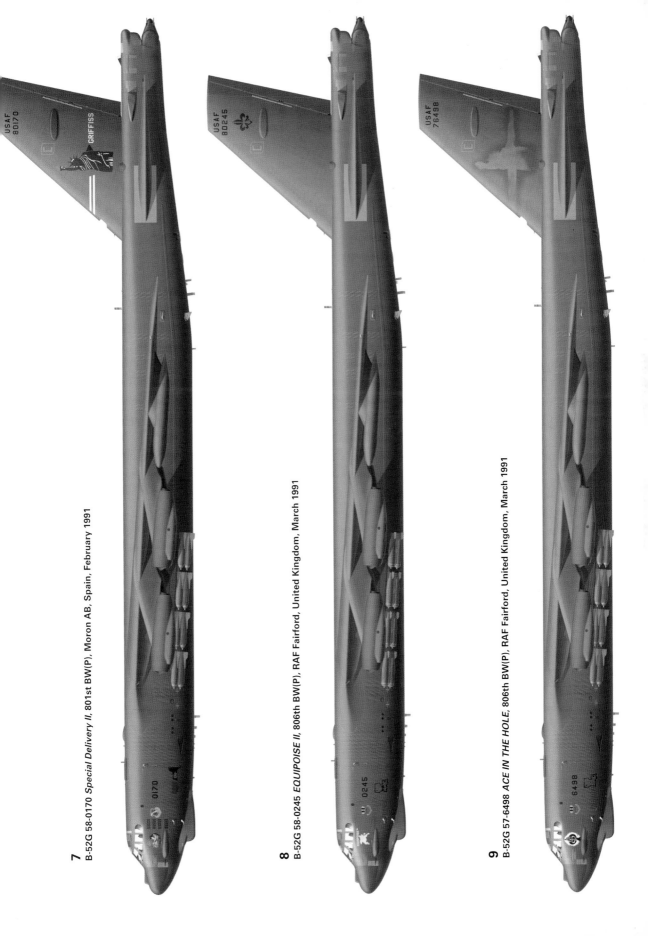

7
B-52G 58-0170 *Special Delivery II*, 801st BW(P), Moron AB, Spain, February 1991

8
B-52G 58-0245 *EQUIPOISE II*, 806th BW(P), RAF Fairford, United Kingdom, March 1991

9
B-52G 57-6498 *ACE IN THE HOLE*, 806th BW(P), RAF Fairford, United Kingdom, March 1991

10
B-52G 58-0168 *Treasure Hunter*, 801st BW(P), Moron AB, Spain, January 1991

11
B-52G 58-0182 *What's Up DOC?*, 806th BW(P), RAF Fairford, United Kingdom, February 1991

12
B-52G 58-0204 *Special Delivery*, 806th BW(P), RAF Fairford, United Kingdom, February 1991

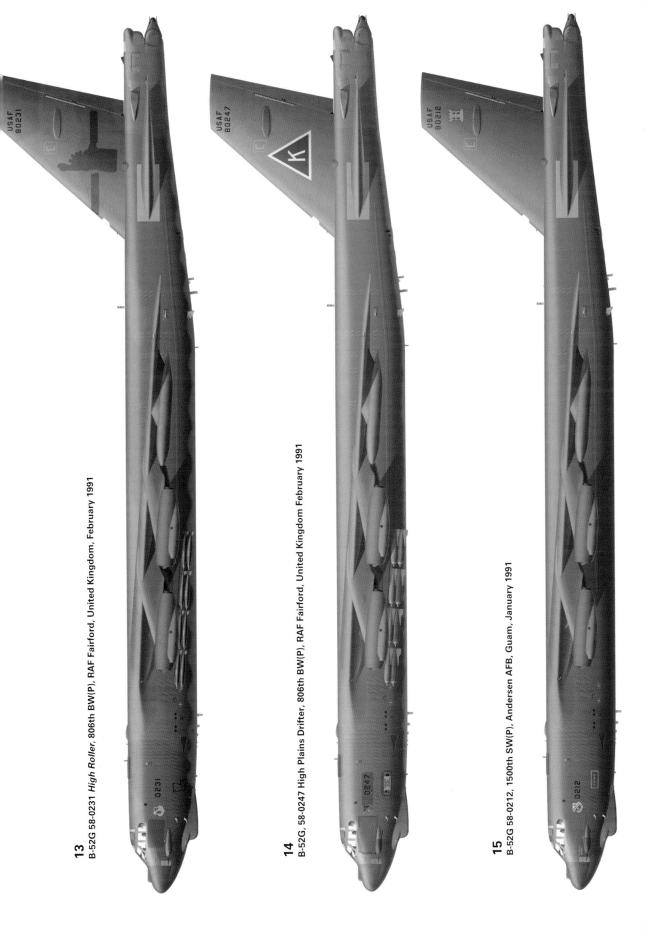

13
B-52G 58-0231 *High Roller*, 806th BW(P), RAF Fairford, United Kingdom, February 1991

14
B-52G, 58-0247 High Plains Drifter, 806th BW(P), RAF Fairford, United Kingdom February 1991

15
B-52G 58-0212, 1500th SW(P), Andersen AFB, Guam, January 1991

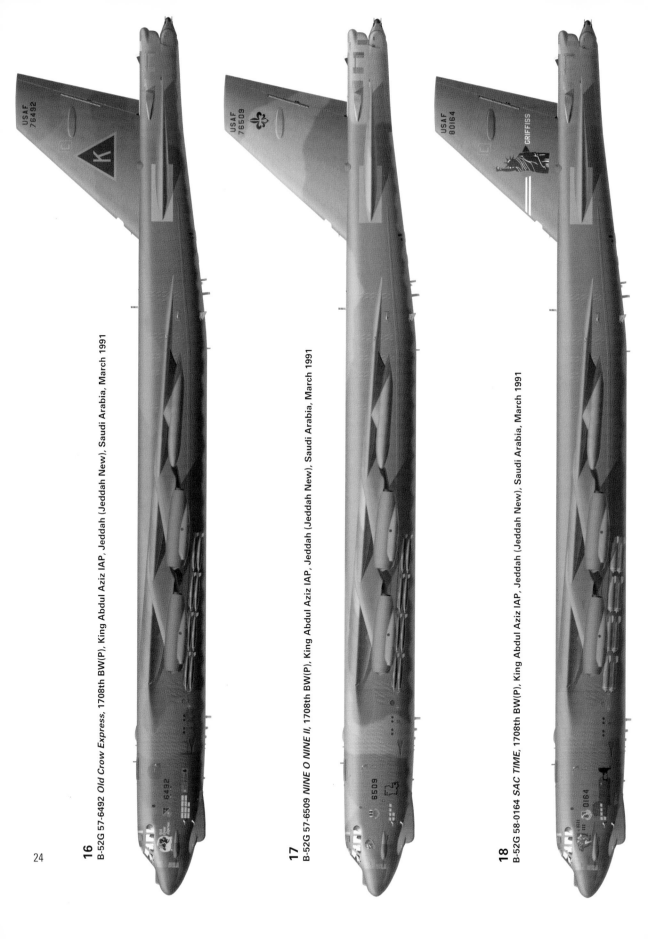

16
B-52G 57-6492 *Old Crow Express*, 1708th BW(P), King Abdul Aziz IAP, Jeddah (Jeddah New), Saudi Arabia, March 1991

17
B-52G 57-6509 *NINE O NINE II*, 1708th BW(P), King Abdul Aziz IAP, Jeddah (Jeddah New), Saudi Arabia, March 1991

18
B-52G 58-0164 *SAC TIME*, 1708th BW(P), King Abdul Aziz IAP, Jeddah (Jeddah New), Saudi Arabia, March 1991

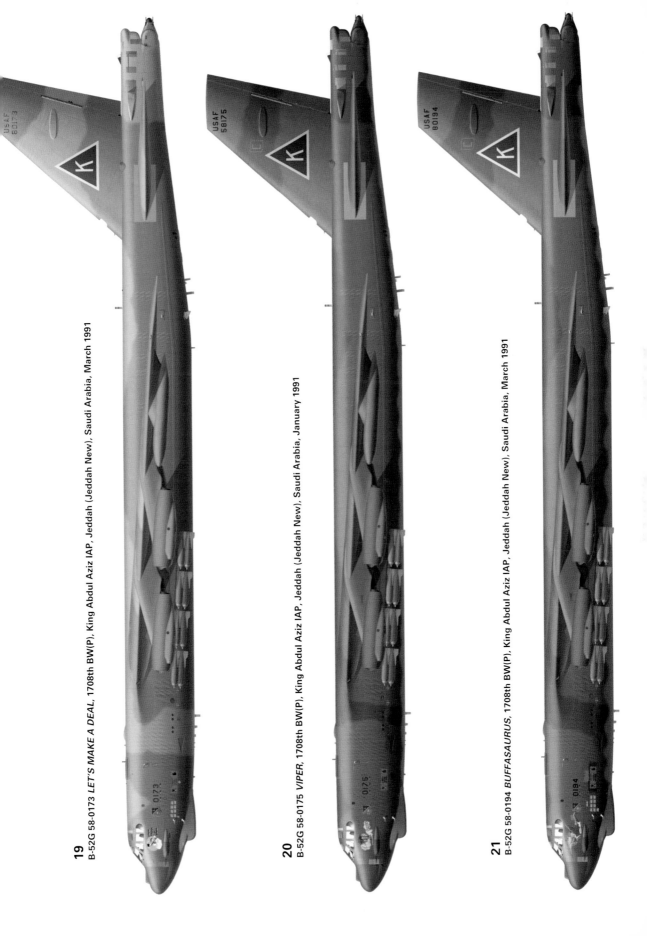

19
B-52G 58-0173 *LET'S MAKE A DEAL*, 1708th BW(P), King Abdul Aziz IAP, Jeddah (Jeddah New), Saudi Arabia, March 1991

20
B-52G 58-0175 *VIPER*, 1708th BW(P), King Abdul Aziz IAP, Jeddah (Jeddah New), Saudi Arabia, January 1991

21
B-52G 58-0194 *BUFFASAURUS*, 1708th BW(P), King Abdul Aziz IAP, Jeddah (Jeddah New), Saudi Arabia, March 1991

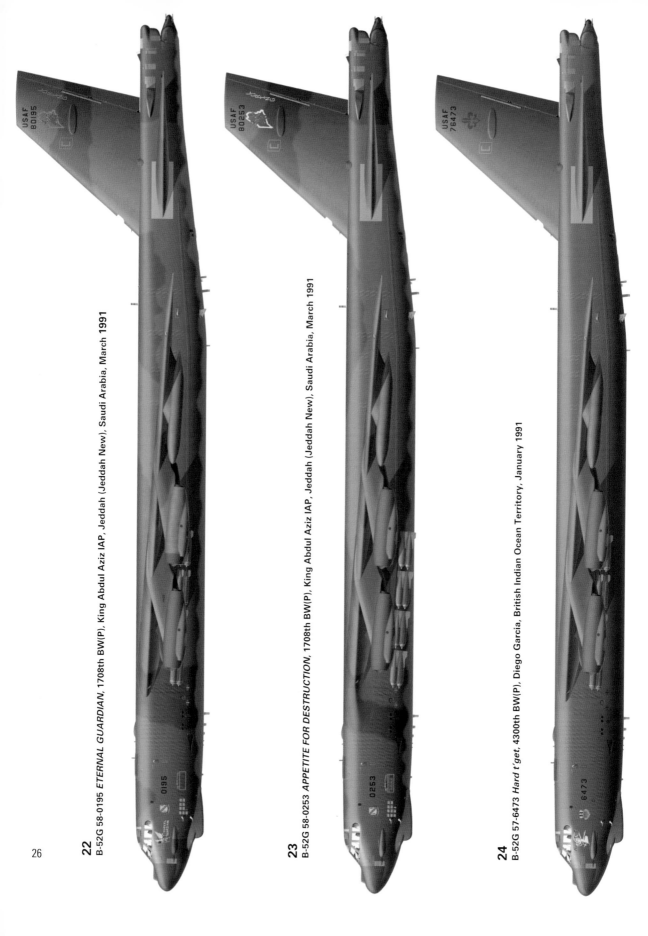

22
B-52G 58-0195 *ETERNAL GUARDIAN*, 1708th BW(P), King Abdul Aziz IAP, Jeddah (Jeddah New), Saudi Arabia, March **1991**

23
B-52G 58-0253 *APPETITE FOR DESTRUCTION*, 1708th BW(P), King Abdul Aziz IAP, Jeddah (Jeddah New), Saudi Arabia, March **1991**

24
B-52G 57-6473 *Hard t'get*, 4300th BW(P), Diego Garcia, British Indian Ocean Territory, January 1991

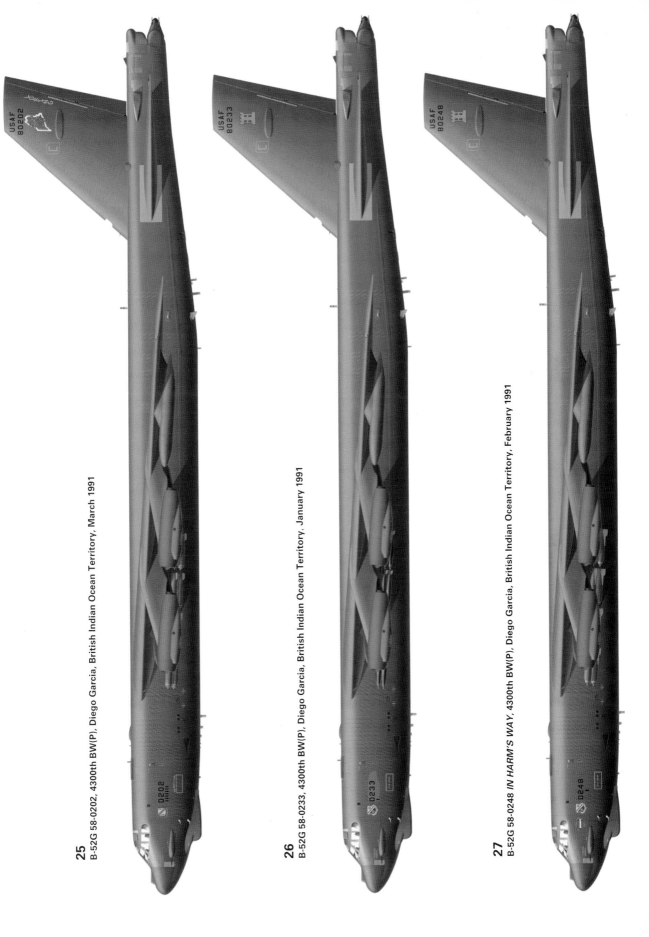

25
B-52G 58-0202, 4300th BW(P), Diego Garcia, British Indian Ocean Territory, March 1991

26
B-52G 58-0233, 4300th BW(P), Diego Garcia, British Indian Ocean Territory, January 1991

27
B-52G 58-0248 *IN HARM'S WAY*, 4300th BW(P), Diego Garcia, British Indian Ocean Territory, February 1991

ETERNAL GUARDIAN

ÆTHERA NOBIS

BUFFASAURUS

019

SPAIN   TEXAS

The Moose is Loose

ÆTHERA NOBIS

0253

Hard Six

The Moose is Loose
Part II
APPETITE FOR DESTRUCTION
C/C SSGT RAFFIAXI
A/C/C A1C XOGIEK

LOLAS

IN HARMS WAY

0248

GRIFFISS

USAF
80253

LORING

USAF
80248

USAF
76473

PRELUDE TO *DESERT STORM*

When the air raids which inaugurated Operation *Desert Storm* commenced on the evening of 16 January 1991, it was widely assumed that all had been launched from bases in the region, especially in Saudi Arabia and Bahrain, and from aircraft carriers sailing in the Persian Gulf and the Red Sea.

In fact, the first offensive sorties of *Desert Storm* had been launched 15 hours earlier when B-52s took off from Barksdale AFB, Louisiana, to begin what would become the longest bombing mission in history.

This first mission of *Desert Storm* remained highly classified for almost a year after the war ended, even though the raid had been a triumphant success, and had marked a historic achievement for the USAF. The mission was not celebrated, or even described, at the time, and the seven B-52 crews who participated were warned not to talk about what they had done. When details were finally revealed to the press and public, it was mentioned apparently 'off-handedly' in a Department of Defense press conference. It has since been claimed that the mission was the longest-ranging combat operation in the history of aerial warfare.

The secrecy surrounding the mission was imposed because the aircraft involved had made the first use of a new and secret weapon, which had been funded and developed under the same 'black world' conditions as the F-117 Stealth Fighter.

This weapon, developed under strict secrecy four years before, was the AGM-86C Conventional Air-launched Cruise Missile (CALCM), code-named *Senior Surprise*. At the time, even this code-name was restricted, and so B-52 crews called it *Secret Squirrel* – a popular cartoon character, who fortuitously shared the same initials!

B-52G 58-0204 (the former *Rivet Ace* testbed) was used as a cruise missile testbed, carrying the Boeing AGM-86B ALCM during the 1979 Joint Cruise Missile Program Fly-off. In this photograph, the aircraft shows how six ALCMs fit onto a B-52's underwing pylon (*Author's collection*)

31

The AGM-86C was designed in the aftermath of Operation *El Dorado Canyon* – the USAF's April 1986 attack against Libya. *El Dorado Canyon* had thrown up a number of problems. While US Navy aircraft participating in the operation had operated from aircraft carriers only a few hundred miles away in the Mediterranean, the USA's NATO allies in southern Europe had been reluctant to allow the USA to launch this controversial operation

Here, 58-0204 is seen carrying the General Dynamics AGM-109 ALCM, which was the unsuccessful design in the USAF's Joint Cruise Missile Program (*Author's collection*)

from their bases. The F-111s used in the attack had therefore been launched from bases in the UK, where host nation support had been easy to obtain.

The Spanish and French governments had even refused to let the bombers over-fly their territories, forcing the F-111 crews to fly an extraordinary route out over the Bay of Biscay and the eastern Atlantic, through the Straits of Gibraltar and across the western Mediterranean. This in turn dictated a heavy reliance on tanker support, and resulted in severe crew fatigue.

The F-111s had been forced to over-fly their targets to drop their laser-guided bombs, and this had required dedicated ECM, SEAD and fighter support. Despite this, one aircraft was shot down, while targeting had proved difficult, and there had been collateral damage, with the killing and injuring of scores of innocent people.

Similar operations in the early 1980s in Lebanon and Grenada had been dominated by US Navy aircraft carriers, and as the Cold War started to wind down, a new era began to unfold in which larger numbers of small-scale regional conflicts seemed increasingly likely. The USAF saw that its power projection role might diminish, with a consequent problem in maintaining its budget in the face of inevitable post-Cold War defence cuts.

In an effort to give the Air Force greater 'global reach' in its conventional power projection role, the Pentagon directed the USAF to find a way to be able to hit similar future targets with less reliance on allied support and tanker assets. The USAF would need to be able to attack such targets more surgically, and from a stand-off range which would reduce vulnerability. Timescale and cost constraints meant that any new precision-guided long-range stand-off missile would best be derived from an existing weapon, and that it would have to be carried by an existing platform. The Pentagon requirement would clearly best be served by using larger strategic bombers such as the B-52 (which had been designed specifically for long-range operations) to deliver the new weapon.

It soon became clear that the nuclear-armed AGM-86B ALCM would form an ideal basis for the new conventional stand-off weapon, and, within three months of the Libya raid, the development of a conventional version of the missile had been launched.

Flying during *Desert Storm* as
What's Up DOC?, B-52G 58-0182 had
previously served with the Air Force
Flight Test Center as *Snowbird*. This
photograph shows the aircraft
launching an early ALCM test round
from its bomb-bay
(*Author's collection*)

Instead of building new missiles, the USAF chose to convert some of the existing 1739 AGM-86Bs to the new conventional configuration. Boeing, as the original manufacturer of the missile, was contracted to perform the conversion work. The W80 nuclear warhead was replaced with a conventional 1000-lb blast fragmentation warhead (which had the same Net Explosive Effect as a conventional 2000-lb bomb), and the ALCM's terrain contour matching guidance system was swapped for a GPS satellite navigation system. This halved the weapon's CEP (circle of equal probabilities) from 30 to 15 metres.

Each AGM-86C conversion cost $380,000, and the resulting weapon was about 650 lbs heavier than the original AGM-86B. The missile had a range of between 600 and 1080 nautical miles. Flight testing began in August 1987, and a year later the CALCM was declared operational. Some 105 Block 0 AGM-86Cs were delivered between 1986 and 1994, about 36 of which had arrived at Barksdale by the time *Desert Storm* began.

Access to the CALCM had been kept 'to an absolute minimum', according to Col Jay Beard, CO of the 596th BS, and only one crew (who had flight-tested the weapon) was available for operations. 'There were just two of us briefed into the programme initially', said Maj Blaise Martinick of Crew S-92, who flew as B-52G 58-0183 *Valkyrie's* radar navigator on the historic mission.

'My friend and I were the only two radars briefed into the *Senior Surprise* programme when Iraq went into Kuwait. We were tasked to develop a plan to carry the CALCM, and because this was a weapon that didn't exist, we were required to plan the mission to begin and end at Barksdale AFB. Our original plan called for 36 CALCM on three bombers, with four air refuelling points strategically positioned. You have to remember that at this time, the 49th Test and Evaluation Squadron was still testing the CALCM, and it had not yet been operationally fielded. Then we eventually briefed in a pilot to help us determine how much air refuelling we would need to get over there, do a mission and get back.'

Strict secrecy was was enforced in order to ensure that the CALCMs would be a complete surprise if they were ever employed, and to avoid complicating the strategic arms control agreements then being finalised with the USSR. Surprise would be vital, since few GPS satellites were then in operation, and their positions were predictable. This meant that in many areas of the globe there would be distinct 'windows' when attacks using GPS-guided weapons might be more likely.

Nevertheless, when Iraqi forces invaded Kuwait on 2 August 1990, the weapon was put 'on alert', as Lt Gen 'Buster' Glosson later recalled. 'We stood them up on alert because we were trying to give the national command authorities some options, and at that point in time there weren't that many other options available for any action the President might have wanted to take.'

US forces in the Middle East were small, and even after being reinforced by deployments, they were initially inadequate to deter (or if necessary repel) any Iraqi invasion of Saudi Arabia, let alone to force or intimidate the Iraqis to retreat from Kuwait. The limited number of CALCMs did offer the USAF the ability to make what Glosson later called 'a useful political statement', however.

Air Force leaders advised the National Security Council that CALCMs would be available for use against Iraq's command, control and communications nodes, as well as its electrical grid, and other high-value targets. In order to achieve this, however, more crews would be needed. In just a few weeks, 15 crews were introduced to the *Secret Squirrel* programme, and seven of these were selected to give the weapon its baptism of fire.

Although the B-52G normally carried a crew of six, it was quickly decided that the *Secret Squirrel* aircraft would have a crew of eight, with a 'pilot augmentee' and a 'navigator augmentee' to permit some rotation of aircrew in order to allow the pilot, co-pilot and primary navigators to rest. Instructor seats were removed from the mission aircraft and air mattresses and sleeping bags were installed – one 'upstairs' and one 'downstairs'.

On the lower deck, the cramped conditions forced anyone using the makeshift bed to make an unfortunate choice. 'One could lie down with either one's head or boots in the urinal', a crewmember later observed. Nor were the bunks particularly comfortable, as Steve Hess, Radar Navigator on 59-2464 'Doom 32', later explained. 'It wasn't really sleeping, it was more like lying down and dehydrating for two hours.' On the day of the mission, one aircraft (58-0183 *Valkyrie*, with Crew S-92) even carried two additional pilots, taking the total to nine!

Seven B-52Gs were selected for the mission, and as soon as sufficient weapons were available, each of the aircraft was loaded with seven CALCMs. The aircraft were kept fully fuelled, and new mission planning tapes with updated targets and weapons-aiming algorithms arrived from SAC headquarters at Offutt AFB, Nebraska, sometimes several times per week.

Whereas B-52s configured for the SIOP carried six AGM-86Bs under each wing, the *Secret Squirrel* aircraft sortied with an asymmetric loadout of three missiles under one wing and four under the other. Col Beard soon began to get calls about the oddly loaded bombers on the

Although no photographs exist of the *Secret Squirrel* aircraft during their historic mission, some of the AGM-86C launches must have looked very much like this (*Author's collection*)

alert pad, and he deflected these by telling the sharp-eyed callers that the unit was practising sortie generation.

The crews continued to stand 'Alpha' (SIOP) alert, in addition to being kept 'on a very short string' for a strike on Iraq, which Col Beard dubbed 'Sierra' alert. As many 2nd BW B-52 crews moved to forward bases in Spain and Diego Garcia, the load on those left at Barksdale increased. 'We were stretched very, very thin', Col Beard observed.

But as the massive build-up of forces in the Middle East continued, the immediate danger of an Iraqi invasion of Saudi Arabia receded, and the chances of a single stand-alone strike reduced. Gen Merrill A McPeak, then Air Force Chief of Staff explained that:

'There was some early exposure. If Saddam Hussein had continued immediately in the direction of Riyadh, we could have had a problem on our hands. But very quickly after the beginning of *Desert Shield*, we had forces in place that could stop any further Iraqi move down the road toward Riyadh. After about the first week, our vulnerability was closed. Any further advance on Saudi Arabia would have been stopped, and we wouldn't have needed that long-range kind of strike.'

Instead, US air commanders began to study how the CALCMs could be integrated into the broader *Desert Storm* air campaign. There was no immediate military requirement to stage a hugely expensive CALCM operation from bases in the United States, although senior USAF officers were keen to do so in order to demonstrate the capacity of the USAF to project military power on a global scale.

It soon became apparent that a gap might emerge immediately following the initial strikes, as the first wave of Coalition aircraft recovered to their bases. Rather than grant Iraq a brief respite Gens McPeak and Glosson decided that the CALCM could fill the gap 'quite nicely', arriving over their targets at precisely the right moment in the mid-morning lull, soon after the first wave had departed. This would keep the intensity of attacks fairly high during the opening hours, thus maintaining the pressure on the Iraqi defences.

At that time CALCMs only carried a 1000-lb fragmentation warhead, so eight soft targets were chosen for the opening attack. These did not require the use of penetrating weapons, and included power stations at Mosul, a telephone exchange in Basra and other electrical-generating facilities. The CALCMs were not sent against targets in Baghdad because this was the first time that GPS guidance had been used by cruise missiles, and there was doubt as to accuracy.

There was more confidence in the Tomahawk land attack missile, which used terrain contour matching (TERCOM) for navigation. Blaise Martinick suggested that, 'Somewhere up the chain of command, the total number of targets (aim points) became 39, and it was decided that it would be better to spread the wealth and increase the number of bombers to seven – therefore, "all of our eggs would not be in the same basket" if you will. Actually, if I remember correctly, the original buy was only 57 CALCMs, and 11 had been used in testing, which left 46.'

Electronic warfare officer (EWO) Maj Todd Mathes, who flew on the mission, was one of the first to be briefed on the operation. He recalled, 'When we were first called in, we were all under the impression that we were going to be launched fairly quickly.' When no mission was launched immediately, many began to doubt whether the *Secret Squirrels* would ever be used.

Another early member of the programme was Maj Marcus Myers, a pilot who flew one of the seven *Secret Squirrel* aircraft. 'Week after week we would study and brief the wing commander on a regular basis, but I don't think any of us thought we were going to do it.'

Col Beard finally received the order he had been waiting for at midnight on 16 January, and the *Secret Squirrel* aircrew were called in. At 0300 hrs a tannoy announcement echoed throughout the alert facility – 'All Sierra crews report to the vault.'

As the aircrew arrived in the 'vault' for their final brief, they were greeted by the sight of the squadron commander, the wing commander and Lt Gen Ellie G 'Buck' Shuler Jr, commander of the Eighth Air Force, and it suddenly hit home 'that those aeroplanes out there were cocked and loaded with real live bombs, and that we were really going to war', Col Beard later recalled.

Gen Shuler told the crews how important their mission was, and compared them to the 'Doolittle Raiders'. 'He hammered home that this was the real deal', said Valkyrie's navigator, Blaise Martinick. 'We're going to go do what we've been trained to do.'

Before the crews 'walked' there was some last minute admin for Col Beard. Some crew members had inexplicably failed to complete wills, and Colonel Beard had to get the base Judge Advocate General out of bed to help complete the task.

To maintain security, or what Beard called a 'low operational signature', it was not possible to open up the dining hall or order up extra boxed meals in order to avoid 'giving the game away' to the kitchen. Instead, some 'meals fit-for-flight' were pre-positioned aboard the jets, together with five-gallon containers of water and 'jugs of tepid coffee'. The meals were low-residue, low-gas versions of the standard US military MRE (meal, ready-to-eat), and were a poor substitute for a square meal, although most of the crews were too pumped up to care.

This photograph has often been described as showing one of the *Secret Squirrel* aircraft during the mission. It does not, but it is perhaps the best representation of how the aircraft would have appeared (*Author's collection*)

Security was a real concern, and on the Air Tasking Order, the ordnance carried by the Barksdale B-52Gs was listed simply as 'XLRBs' (extra-long-range bombs) to obscure the identity of the CALCMs.

More seriously, the take-off time was put back for security reasons. Gen Glosson worried that Libya might spot the B-52s on radar and warn Iraq that an attack force was inbound. The CALCM mission was therefore rescheduled so that the B-52s would not pass Libya until after the F-117s had hit their first targets in Baghdad.

Using the call-signs 'Doom 31' to 'Doom 37', the seven B-52Gs took off armed with the 39 available AGM-86Cs. Radar navigator Blaise Martinick remembered that, 'Four of the aircraft were loaded with six missiles and three aircraft were loaded with five missiles, although the G-model was capable of carrying 12 missiles. I'm not really sure how the final load out was determined.'

This put the aircraft close to their maximum permitted take-off weights, and heavier than most of the pilots had ever flown at 244 tons, and they needed more than 9000 ft of Barksdale's rain-soaked runway to struggle into the air.

On board 59-5282 *Grim Reaper II*, co-pilot Capt (now Lt Col) Warren Ward looked down at his old school as he climbed away from Barksdale. 'I'm a graduate of Louisiana Tech, and on the way out, as the sun was coming up, I could see Wylie Tower down at Ruston, and I remember thinking "Am I ever gonna see that again?" It was one of the thoughts running through my mind.'

The planned route took the loose gaggle of B-52Gs out over the eastern United States, across the north Atlantic, over southern Europe, the Mediterranean and Egypt, and finally into the planned launch area over western Saudi Arabia.

As the B-52Gs neared their first air-to-air refuelling rendezvous, near the Azores, Col Beard, on board lead bomber 58-0177 *PETIE 3RD* (call-sign 'Doom 31'), contacted the other aircraft on secure frequencies and asked them to check in. 57-6475 *MIAMI Clipper II* (call-sign 'Doom 34') did not check in, and all Beard heard from Capt Bernie Morgan and co-pilot Lt Mike Branch on board the jet was a terse, 'We're working something right now, and we'll get back to you.'

Michael Branch was an extraordinary young African American, who had completed pilot training at Vance AFB, Oklahoma, as recently as July 1988, but who was not destined to live long after the mission. A prominent soccer coach and athlete, and a proud member of the East Coast Chapter of the Tuskegee Airmen, Branch was also a volunteer Literacy Tutor, determined to ensure that other African Americans could fulfil their potential. He died of cancer on 29 December 1993 at the Malcolm Grow Medical Center, Andrews AFB.

Only after exceeding the point at which any aircraft could turn back did Morgan and Branch admit that they had shut down an engine on take-off due to fluctuating oil pressure. Strictly speaking, this should have led them to abort the mission, but it had been determined that a B-52 could complete the mission with just six of its eight engines, and the crew of 'Doom 34' were determined not to be left behind.

'They did exactly what I would have done – I expected nothing less. I wanted them to be gung ho', Col Beard commented later.

The seven B-52Gs refuelled from a group of KC-135s sortied from Lajes Field, on the Azores. Strict radio silence was observed, but the KC-135 crews found their own ways to wish their thirsty customers 'godspeed'. On board 58-0238 *Miss Fit II* ('Doom 35'), aircraft commander Capt Marcus Myers recalled that, 'Up in the boom pod window, they held up a sign that said, "Good hunting". So even though they weren't sure what we were doing, they had an idea.'

The bombers refuelled again over the Mediterranean, this time from KC-10 Extenders operating from Moron AB, Spain. There was no indication that the jets were detected by the Libyans, although there were some inconclusive radar contacts that led Capt Steve Hess, radar navigator on board 59-2564 'Doom 32', to suspect otherwise. 'We thought somebody might have come up to look us over', he said later.

Capt Todd Mathes, the EWO on board *Miss Fit II*, was able to identify whose radar was painting the B-52s. 'The Soviet navy knew we were there because they were lighting us up pretty good, but we had to actually see a missile in the air before we could react.' Using the 'Buffs' powerful on-board jammers would have announced the bombers' presence, so the crews stuck to their flight plan, which had been carefully and exhaustively planned to deconflict the B-52s with other allied combat aircraft and commercial air traffic.

After crossing the Mediterranean, the Red Sea and the Arabian Desert, the crews began to arm their missiles before starting their run ins to the launch point – 60 miles south of the Iraqi–Saudi border near the town of Ar Ar – all while flying lights-out and in radio silence.

As the crews ran through their pre-attack procedures, it became clear that four missiles were having software problems. Because strict orders had been issued not to launch missiles unless they were completely 'serviceable', these four weapons could not be used in an effort to avoid collateral damage.

The remaining 35 CALCMs were launched according to a carefully planned sequence over a ten-minute period. The missile launch times were planned so that they all arrived at their targets simultaneously, and so that they did not collide on launch.

'We literally launched the first weapons of *Desert Storm*', said Kirkpatrick, later, although some maintain that they did not, since they were timed to launch *after* the F-117s had gone in.

Blaise Martinick recalled 'a moment of excitement in launching, but then there's also a moment of remorse, because what we're doing could, and most probably will, cause death. And that is something that everyone has to think about, and has in their mind.'

According to some sources, 33 of the 35 missiles fired struck their targets, although others suggest that 31 of the CALCMs hit their targets. One missile's Williams F107 turbofan engine failed on release from the B-52, and it fell intact in the launch area, where it later had to be found and destroyed to prevent its capture by the enemy. Another missile failed to explode when it hit the target, and a third was never accounted for – it may have been shot down.

Bomb-damage assessment was difficult throughout *Desert Storm*, and this particularly applied to the CALCM strikes. Reconnaissance showed that some of the missiles had hit their targets with incredible

An AGM-86B separates from the underwing pylon of a B-52G test aircraft, the weapon's wings and tail fins already starting to unfold, and its jet engine about to fire up into life (*Author's collection*)

precision, one snapping its telephone pole aim-point in half. Gen Glosson noted that, 'The next night, when the sun set, the lights didn't come on in Iraq. It was clear that either the B-52s were very successful or the Iraqis turned off a lot of power. As we found out later, it was a combination of both.'

The raid was ultimately assessed as having achieved between 85 and 91 per cent of its objectives – considerably better than the expected 80 per cent success rate.

When the last missile had been launched, the B-52Gs turned west for home, although their mission was far from over. Flying east, the bombers had benefited from a tailwind, but now they had to fly into the same wind on the return journey. 'The anticipation was gone, as was our tailwind, so the return flight was much longer, both physically and mentally', recalled Todd Mathes, EWO on *Miss Fit II*.

This had an obvious implication for fuel consumption, which was also going to be affected by unserviceabilities – two aircraft were flying with seized engines or seized pairs of engines, significantly increasing drag, and two more B-52s were experiencing fluctuating oil pressure readings. Four of the aircraft were also carrying heavy, high drag, unlaunched missiles. Together, these problems required additional, unscheduled refuelling sorties to enable the B-52s to complete the journey back to Barksdale AFB.

The return flight was also disrupted by severe weather. With only 30 minutes of fuel remaining in some cases, the crews encountered poor visibility over the Mediterranean, threatening the much needed first aerial refuelling contact. Fortunately, conditions improved enough for the B-52Gs to refuel from Moron-based KC-10s.

As the bombers headed across the Atlantic, they encountered 130- to 140-knot headwinds, when the worst-case planning assumption had been a headwind of just 90 knots. Col Beard tried changing altitude, but the winds were equally severe, and more bad news came when it was learned that the wind at Lajes was so strong that the base's KC-135 tankers had been grounded!

In a frantic effort to avoid diverting to a European airfield with aircraft carrying what looked like nuclear weapons, Col Beard radioed Moron AB, who scrambled a flight of KC-10s which stayed with the bombers for as long as they could. This was enough to ensure that the

The two unique crew patches worn by *Secret Squirrel* participants after the mission had been officially revealed in late 1992

aircraft could get back across the Atlantic, although continuing headwinds and drag caused by 'hung' missiles meant that some jets would have to divert to east coast airfields without a further 'top-up'.

Col Beard was determined that none of his B-52s would have to land unannounced at an east coast base carrying their top-secret weapons, and he ensured that two 'strip tankers' were launched from Robins AFB, Georgia. One of the bombers had a radio fault and was unable to communicate with the tanker, so Beard stayed with it, talking to the 'Buff' pilot and relaying messages to the tanker.

On landing, the B-52s reportedly taxied directly into their shelters, in order to expose the unlaunched missiles to as few eyes as possible. The crews finally went 'off-duty' after a perfunctory debrief.

Total secrecy surrounded this mission, and the participating crews were ordered not to tell anyone about what they had done. Capt Steven W Kirkpatrick, augmentee pilot on 58-0185 *El Lobo II*, recalled that, 'My wife wanted to know where I had been, but I couldn't say anything.' Marcus Myers, captain of *Miss Fit II*, remembered that, 'It was tough to not talk about it. People knew we were doing something, but they didn't know we were doing a CALCM strike.'

Blaise Martinick remembered that, 'For a year we had to listen to the F-117 "pointy-nosed" boys bragging about how they were the first in Iraq, and the first to strike targets during the war. But the day our mission was declassified it was quickly realised that the "Buffs" were the first in, and also the first to strike targets, and the F-117s followed the CALCM weapons. What a great slap in the face that was for the fighter boys.'

Finally, almost a year after the mission, the classification was removed, and the story of the operation was casually revealed during a routine press conference. Each participating crewmember was awarded an Air Medal, and they were finally allowed to tell their story.

The citations accompanying the Air Medals spoke of their historic and unprecedented demonstration of the Air Force's philosophy of 'Global Reach, Global Power'.

Gen Glosson and other senior officers held up the operation as a conclusive demonstration of the flexible, expeditionary capability of American air power, but denied that the CALCM raid had been mounted merely as a stunt intended to advertise the USAF's ability to mount a long-range strike from the American heartland. Glosson said that, 'It's incredible what people say in hindsight. Had my interest been to just demonstrate a new capability, I would have done it two or three times, and not kept the programme secret afterwards. We used those weapons because it seemed the logical thing to do. Plain and simple, because it saved lives. If we had lost a half-dozen A-6 Intruders attacking those same targets, it would have been unforgivable.'

Historically, Operation *Senior Surprise* was a milestone, marking the first time that bombers had taken off from the continental United States to strike a target half way around the world. Some saw it as marking the start of a shift away from maintaining a 'forward presence' of US combat forces, to an era that would be characterised by Stateside basing of forces that would be configured for rapid deployment and expeditionary action.

More obviously, the 14,000-mile, 34.5-hour round-trip mission set endurance and range records for an operational bombing mission, smashing earlier records set during Vietnam's Operation *Linebacker* and the RAF's *Black Buck* Vulcan attacks during the Falklands War. Interestingly, a pilot who flew nine *Desert Storm* missions from Diego Garcia later broke the record set by the *Secret Squirrel* B-52s.

Maj Mel Deaile joined the B-2 programme in 1998, and helped plan the bomber's first combat strikes in support of Operation *Allied Force* in Kosovo in March 1999. Subsequently, Deaile led a formation of B-2s on a 44-hour mission to Afghanistan, which overtook *Senior Surprise* to become the longest combat mission in aviation history.

The *Secret Squirrel* mission was not enough to save the 596th BS from oblivion. The unit converted to 'LA'-coded B-52Hs in 1992, but was disbanded in October 1993, being re-numbered as the 62nd BS.

Most of the seven B-52Gs which participated in the operation were quickly retired to the MASDC 'boneyard' at Davis-Monthan, although two of the *Secret Squirrel* B-52Gs (58-0183 *Valkyrie* and 58-0185 *El Lobo II*) escaped parts reclamation and scrapping. *Valkyrie* is on display at the Pima County Air Museum on Davis-Monthan's perimeter, while *El Lobo II* is displayed at the Air Force Armament Museum at Eglin Air Force Base, Florida.

Six of the seven *Secret Squirrel* aircraft wore nose art. 57-6475 was *MIAMI Clipper II*, 58-0177 was *PETIE 3RD*, 58-0183 was *Valkyrie*, 58-0185 was *El Lobo II*, 58-0238 was *Miss Fit II* and 59-2582 was *Grim Reaper II* (*Andy Bloom*)

FIRE FROM THE ISLAND

The first B-52G bombers deployed for Operation *Desert Shield* were assigned to the newly formed 17th Air Division (Provisional) and were based at Diego Garcia, a British dependency in the Chagos Archipelago, British Indian Ocean Territory. Diego Garcia is a lush, jungle-covered 17-square-mile atoll of coral and sand in the middle of the Indian Ocean, the southernmost of 52 such islands in the archipelago.

Until 1976, the British Indian Ocean Territory (BIOT) and Diego Garcia were under the administrative control of the British government of the Seychelles, which then gained independence. The BIOT became a self-administering territory under direct control of the East African Desk of the British Foreign Office The island had been uninhabited until colonial workers arrived on the island in the late 19th and early 20th centuries – some 1200 to 2000 of these 'Ilois' were moved off the island to Mauritius in the late 1960s. Although they had lived on Diego Garcia for several generations, the British and American government prefer to view the 'Ilois' as temporary workers rather than indigenous inhabitants, thus giving them no right of return. This lack of indigenous inhabitants has increased the island's usefulness as a secure and secret military base.

Diego Garcia was developed as a joint Anglo-American naval and aircraft refuelling and support station and radar and radio post during the 1960s and 1970s, with massive improvements to the island's airfield and port infrastructure. After the commissioning of a US Naval Communication Station in 1973, the airfield's 8000-ft runway was extended to 12,000 ft, and a ship channel and turning basin was constructed in the lagoon. The island's facilities were further improved and expanded during the 1980s.

Located in the middle of the Indian Ocean, outside the cyclone area, Diego Garcia was ideal for monitoring Soviet naval activity in the region, and after the fall of the Shah of Iran it provided a useful base for US forces.

Since the end of the Cold War, Diego Garcia has proved pivotal in the support of expeditionary warfare in West Asia and the Middle East. Today, the island is effectively a military camp – a stationary aircraft carrier seven degrees south of the Equator and 1000 miles south of India.

It is the responsibility of the Thirteenth Air Force's Det 1 to operate and maintain a Southwest Asia contingency base on Diego Garcia, providing the facilities, fuel, aerospace ground equipment and munitions required to sustain operations by deployed bombers and tankers.

In the build-up to war, it was felt expedient to base B-52s (which had something of an 'image problem' by dint of their nuclear role and formidable heavy bombing capability) close enough to be able to fight if required, but not so close as to complicate diplomatic negotiations among the USA's Arab and Gulf allies.

From 1 August 1990 to 28 February 1991, the base population of Diego Garcia effectively doubled with the deployment of a Strategic Air Command bombardment wing and other aviation detachments.

The SAC B-52G wing deployed to Diego Garcia was designated as the 4300th BW(P). The wing's first element of seven B-52G bombers were drawn from Loring's 42nd BW, and these deployed on 12 August. The aircraft flew out to Diego Garcia laden with M117R iron bombs, 2400 rounds of cannon ammunition and chaff and flares so that they could be immediately turned around on arrival in-theatre ready for operations.

The 42nd BW, led by Col Terry Burke, was SAC's conventional B-52 wing, and instead of standing hours of Alert duty, its crews routinely deployed overseas. When Iraqi forces invaded Kuwait on 2 August 1990, the 42nd BW had been preparing to return home to Loring AFB from a *Green Flag* exercise at Nellis AFB, Nevada, and so its crews were at the peak of their operational efficiency, with realistic experience of making low-level attacks against desert targets.

The 42nd BW was given only three days' notice to deploy to its forward operating location at Diego Garcia. The wing's first group of B-52s flew non-stop, crossing the Atlantic and Mediterranean (avoiding overflying any country except Gibraltar), before heading south over the Red Sea. The bombers followed a route which ran down the middle of the Red Sea, since both Saudi Arabia and Egypt had refused the diplomatic clearance required for overflight of their territory.

As the B-52s began another session of inflight refuelling, the crews were informed that Yemen was preparing to scramble fighters to shoot them down. They were then cleared into Saudi airspace, which they crossed, gaining an exit clearance into oceanic airspace over Oman. The refuelling was terminated, and the bombers were left short of fuel, but they had effectively 'cut the corner'.

The B-52Gs finally crossed the Indian Ocean to Diego Garcia. The flight lasted 20 hours, and each B-52G had to refuel three times from their accompanying KC-10 tankers, taking on 70 tons of fuel each time. 'Everyone was wide awake passing Libya', recalled one 42nd BW veteran. 'We didn't know how Libya would react to seeing B-52s drive past.'

By 16 August the 4300th BW was fully formed with 20 fully armed B-52Gs on alert, including further aircraft from the 42nd BW and more

A line-up of B-52Gs, mainly from Loring's 42nd BW, at Diego Garcia during *Desert Storm*. The nearest aircraft – 59-2572 – flew 14 missions from the base, amassing 190.5 flying hours. As this photograph clearly shows, most of the Diego Garcia aircraft were painted grey overall. The second aircraft in this line-up has SAC's 'Peace is Our Profession' badge on its starboard side (*via Tony Cassanova*)

Diego Garcia, seen from the north-east, looking down the runway's extended centreline. Eclipse Bay lies to the right of the Main Pass, with Orient Bay and Rambler Bay to the left

G-models from the 93rd BW at Castle AFB. Small numbers of aircrew were also posted in from Griffiss and Barksdale AFBs. The 20 Primary Aircraft Authorised officially consisted of 16 from the 42nd and four from the 93rd BWs, and crews from the 97th and 416th BWs. A total of 32 aircraft were eventually deployed (not simultaneously) – 16 each from the 42nd and 93rd BWs – although the peak strength was 24 jets. All were conventional aircraft, colloquially known as '777' jets. These were backed up by KC-135R and KC-10 tankers, as well as a detachment of rescue helicopters.

Although the 4300th BW(P) was one of the largest B-52G provisional units, Diego Garcia's vast distance from the target area meant that its aircraft flew fewer, much longer sorties. Thus, while the 1708th BW(P) at Jeddah flew 841 sorties, totalling 3709.4 hours, the 4300th BW(P) flew only 459 sorties, totalling 6525.4 hours. The latter wing dropped 18,411 weapons (of the 72,289 delivered by B-52Gs during *Desert Storm*, comprising 10,398 M117s, 6225 Mk 82s and 287 UK 1000-lb bombs – aircraft flying from Diego Garcia and Moron routinely used this weapon. The 4300th BW(P) delivered fewer CBUs than the Jeddah and Moron detachments – 360 CBU-52s, 979 CBU-58s and 162 CBU-71/87/89s.

The 42nd BW's 58-0197 flew 17 missions with the 4300th BW(P), totalling 254.8 flying hours. Every mission from Diego Garcia was a gruelling marathon – even the rare few which ended with a landing in-theatre at Jeddah (*Andy Bloom*)

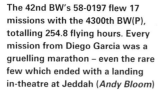

Some 20 B-52Gs are visible in this view of Diego Garcia's airfield, looking north-east towards the viewpoint of the previous photo. The other aircraft seen parked on the ramp are KC-10 and KC-135 tankers. A second major parking apron is visible closer to the runway threshold, but this is empty

The deployed B-52Gs formed a new provisional bomb squadron, and procedures were quickly standardised to allow aircrews sent from different bases to operate together, while aircrew with little exposure to the latest conventional modifications were hastily trained in conventional tactics, techniques and procedures.

A Consolidated Aircraft Maintenance Squadron (CAMS) was formed within the 4300th BW(P), integrating the maintenance and munitions specialists from many bomber bases into one giant, cohesive organisation. Many of the deployed technicians and engineers had never worked on the B-52G, or with conventional weapons, and a training regime was established. Despite the crews' inexperience, the B-52G's mission capable rate actually improved slightly during *Desert Storm*, hitting 82 per cent. This was a tribute to the dedication and hard work of the B-52G groundcrews, many of whom worked 14- to 16-hour days.

Though designed to support deployments, Diego Garcia's facilities were overwhelmed by the influx of more than 3000 aircrew, maintenance personnel, mission planners, security police and other specialists. The visitors' quarters at Diego Garcia immediately filled up, and a huge tent city was erected opposite the B-52 ramp.

Initially, the Diego Garcia-based bombers stood ready to counter any Iraqi invasion of Saudi Arabia. The plan was for the aircraft to operate in their usual low-level role against the invading forces. After about three weeks, this duty passed to A-10 and F-16 units in-theatre, and the B-52s were increasingly tasked against fixed targets in the Air Tasking Order.

As well as flying training sorties, the B-52 crews found plenty to do, 'fishing for tuna and marlin, sailing, windsurfing and beginning a daily ritual of racquetball and fielded teams to augment the Navy's intramural softball league in the evenings', remembered one aircrewman.

Even though the B-52s were deployed to deter possible attacks against Saudi Arabia, such overtly offensive aircraft could not initially be based in Saudi Arabia. Indeed, the Saudi government was initially unwilling to even allow the B-52s to train over its territory, although this restriction was soon lifted.

This was lucky, since the desert nights were sometimes so dark that NVGs and the aircraft's low-light camera proved nearly useless. This became clear during early low-level training sorties, and pilots had to learn to fly a few hundred feet above the sand relying only on the aircraft's terrain-avoidance radar display, while the navigator and radar navigator were glued to the radar altimeter.

During these training missions, the B-52s were regularly bounced by British and American fighters. This provided training for the B-52 gunners, who 'fired' at the 'enemy fighters' while directing the pilots' evasive manoeuvres. When the B-52Gs returned to Diego Garcia, their EWOs practised jamming a 'threat' emitter that had been shipped out especially.

There was a spirited debate among mission planners as to whether to begin the B-52's war by bombing from high or low altitude. Some argued that by attacking from high level, crews would avoid the intense AAA fire that Iraq could throw up, but most preferred low-level bombing, for which the force had trained, and which promised to give better protection against SAMs and enemy fighters.

Pterodactyl Courier of the 42nd BW was one of the most imaginatively named 'Buffs' to see combat in *Desert Storm*, with its nose art showing a Pterodactyl dropping an AGM-84 Harpoon missile. The aircraft flew seven missions from Diego Garcia, totalling just short of 100 hours (*Andy Bloom*)

John Ritter, a 42nd BW pilot who flew with the 4300th BW(P), recalled that, 'We sent representatives up to Riyadh to advise the central air planners on how best to use our aeroplane. We wanted to fly low, preferably at night, protected by fighters and radar jamming aircraft.'

In the end, the planners decided that the B-52s would 'sneak in below radar cover for the first few nights and then go to high bombing when it was safer'. Heavy casualties were expected according to John Ritter. 'Occasionally, we would have a General swing through to tell us how the plan was progressing. "Buster" Glosson told us how they expected as high as 30 per cent casualties at one point for the first night, should it come to pass. Gen Beckel of the Fifteenth Air Force also told us not to test fire the tail guns, as they were prone to mechanical breakdowns. We wondered aloud later whether we would be able to depend on them in combat.

'And they weren't sure we'd be able to get the new Kevlar flak vests [a torso suit] to protect us from shrapnel. After enough clamouring, for lack of a better word, and good work by Col Burke, an interim fix soon arrived – flak vests from Vietnam! They were the old clamshell armour, but were much better than nothing. We were told to keep them, which I did – I still have mine. And right before the war started, the Kevlar suits showed up. On the first night of *Desert Storm*, and for most of my subsequent missions, I wore both. I was just small enough to fit into the ejection seat with both vests on, plus my survival vest, which contained a pistol, rounds and various survival tools – maps, blood chit and water. I figured I was good for almost a 20 mm round.'

Crews began to be briefed on their first-night targets as early as mid-December 1990, and spent the next month memorising the targets, routes and mission timing, and then fine-tuning their planned tactics.

'As the UN deadline of 16 January 1991 approached, and Saddam refused to back down, they cut all open communications from the island. Only secure comms were permitted – guys could no longer even call home', John Ritter remembered.

A well-rehearsed plan swung into action on the evening of 16 January. At 2009 hrs Baghdad time, the 4300th launched 18 aircraft (20 according to some sources). As the first B-52s taxied out and began to take off, hundreds of maintenance troops and spectators lined the taxiways, giving the aircrews a rousing send-off. One maintainer later recalled that, 'We lined up on the side of the maintenance ramp and held our thumbs up to all of the aircrews taxiing for take-off. It was probably the proudest and most patriotic time of my life.'

Eighteen bombers and 13 tankers departed without a single late take-off or abort. Five 'air spares' peeled off and returned to base. Twelve of the 13 remaining B-52Gs reached their targets successfully, the 13th turning back with a malfunction at the Iraqi border.

With 24 missions and 347 flying hours under its belt, 58-0216, seen here immediately after the war, was probably the top-scoring 'Buff' flying from Diego Garcia. The *THUNDER STRUCK* nose art was a post-war addition to the aircraft's colour scheme, but *The Moose is Loose* legend was worn during the war (*Terry Panopalis*)

Six of the B-52s would fly missions and then recover at Jeddah, while the remainder returned to Diego Garcia. The six jets which moved on to Jeddah were themselves replaced by six aircraft from the 1500th Strategic Wing (Provisional) on Guam, as navigator Jim Clonts explained:

'My crew deployed to Andersen AFB on 5 January. We spent the next two weeks flying the 43rd BW B-52 simulator and conducting real "live fire" training missions against a small island nearby. When *Desert Storm* began, we launched from Guam at 0100 hrs and ferried a jet to Diego Garcia, filling the ramp. It was almost a week later before I flew my first combat mission.

'The first three nights, the 4300th crews flew a total of 36 low-level missions, at night, at extremely low altitude, using night vision goggles. Every one of these missions hit their scheduled target, and all jets returned safely to base. One B-52G did have its gun turret blown off by either AAA or a missile. There was a lot of speculation as to what struck the aeroplane, and whether it was enemy or friendly fire. There are a lot of theories, but I don't know what really happened. The pilot, Maj Linwood Mason, who was my Flight Commander, managed to keep the jet under control, and he returned for an emergency landing. He was later decorated for his excellent airmanship.'

A B-52 maintainer known only as 'Twiggley' was able to give more detail as to what happened to the aircraft which lost its tail turret, and landed safely at Jeddah:

'The aircraft (B-52G 58-0248, nicknamed *In Harm's Way*) had the aft six to eight feet of its fuselage blown completely off during the first days of the war. There were – and still are – two different versions of how it ended up in that shape. During a documentary shown on the *Discovery Wings* channel, the aircrew claimed that they were in a very high angle bank when ground fire took the aft section off, gun turret and all.

47

It was a HARM-shooting F-4G Phantom II 'Wild Weasel' like this one which is believed to have caused the damage to B-52G 58-0248. This particular jet is seen disconnecting from the boom of a USAF tanker in a spray of kerosene prior to heading into Iraq during *Desert Storm* (*USAF official*)

'Rumour and popular belief have it that the B-52's gunner turned his defensive fire control systems (DFCS) radar on at exactly the same time as an F-4G "Wild Weasel" shot off an AGM-88 High speed Anti-Radiation Missile (HARM) at a ground threat. The B-52 got in the way of the missile, which was now trained on the DFCS radar emissions.

'At Jeddah, we could clearly see that all the metal shards and jagged edges at the rear of the B-52 were pointing downwards when the damage was viewed from the under-side of the tail section. Perhaps the final clincher in favour of the HARM theory is that SAC and the USAF let us give the bomber the *In Harm's Way* nickname and nose art. That would have had to be one hell of a bank angle – upside down! – for ground fire to have caused that sort of damage.

'I witnessed the damage, along with all the other maintainers on the flightline at Diego Garcia, BIOT, where it landed en route to Guam for repair. Andersen AFB had the only heavy maintenance facility for B-52s in-theatre that could repair that type of extensive damage. It stayed on Guam, unflyable, until the end of the war.

'I, along with more than a few others, volunteered to put her back together immediately after the war by basically sawing off the aft section of another unflyable B-52G that was already on Guam with an unrepairable wing spar break and patching it onto '0248. We accomplished that feat in about seven weeks, patching all the gun-plumbing and other avionics in, and then sent her back to Castle. I flew on that mission back to my, and the aircraft's, home base, and all the operational checkouts en route were code 1 – no defect, fully mission capable. That was my last flight in a B-52, and one I will proudly remember forever. It was also my homecoming from the war.'

The B-52Gs often attacked at very low level, having to pull up in order to turn without 'brushing' a wingtip across the desert floor. Anti-aircraft fire was fierce (if often inaccurate), providing the B-52 pilots with a terrifying firework display. But even the 'Buff's' own weapons could be distracting, as one 4300th BW(P) pilot later recalled:

'The most disorienting thing I've ever done is drop a full load of CBUs at night. We had never done that in training, so the first time I ever dropped a full load of CBUs at low-level at night was in combat – it was incredible. I was not prepared for the amount of light and flash, or how disorienting it was.'

B-52G 58-0248 of the 42nd BW flew just one mission during *Desert Storm*, launching from Diego Garcia, but landing at Jeddah 12 hours later after a 'suspected HARM fratricide'. The aircraft was patched up and ferried back to Guam, via Diego Garcia. It was restored and repaired at Guam, where the B-52 was christened *In Harm's Way* (*Desert Storm Memorial*)

The B-52Gs, A-6Es, F-111Fs and Tornado GR 1s that made low-level attacks during the first days of *Desert Storm* were vulnerable to low-altitude defences – especially AAA and IR-guided SAMs. The switch to medium-altitude attacks was made when the objectives of the low-level bombing campaign were fulfilled, and not because of any fear of unacceptable loss rates, nor because 'no Iraqi target was so important as to justify the loss of a pilot's life', as was sometimes claimed.

Capt John Ritter flew a 'Night One' mission against a dispersal airfield at As Salman, which was also home to a sector operations centre for the Iraqi air defence network and a rear echelon army division. He saw at first hand the impressive Iraqi air defences, but also witnessed the way in which low-level tactics resulted in a zero loss rate:

'The staff briefed "the plan", although it was one we had helped develop, and knew by heart. We'd fly out without filing flight plans and gas up en route, with a top off once we were feet dry over Saudi, entering the peninsula over Oman. Before we got within range of the Iraqi early warning radars, we'd drop to low level and blitz across the border to our target. Each target was to be serviced by three aircraft, hitting in a choreographed multi-axis attack. Lead and No 3 jets dropped British 1000-lb bombs – a new time-delay weapon that buried itself in the dirt and went off sometime in the next 48 hours, thus making it a 1000-lb land mine. These weapons were "laced" over the top by the No 2 jet's CBU-89 Gator mines – anti-personnel and anti-armour "minelets" that made it hazardous for repair crews to search for the big bombs. We'd delouse back across the border and then climb up for the drone home.

'Each route was laid out so we'd all hit our targets within minutes of each other, and cross into Iraq from several points at about the same time. We were to be just a few miles behind the lead wave of fighters en route to Baghdad and Tallil at the "push". At some point, a thought crossed my mind that I'd have to look back on this and remember it for the future, and somehow I knew everything would be alright. Call it Divine Inspiration or whatever you will, I knew we'd be okay beyond a shadow of a doubt. I was able to relax and concentrate on the mission. We reviewed the Combat Search and Rescue plan, made our final coordination briefs and rode out to start our preflights.

'As luck would have it, my crew was to be the last to take off and the first to recover, and that stroke of fate allowed me to witness something I'll never forget. Despite inter-service rivalries, and the competition that resulted from sticking a bunch of Air Force fliers at a Navy base, something very special happened on the ramp that night. As the aircraft launched one by one, the crew chiefs stayed out on the ramp rather than going back to their tents. Navy personnel augmented them until there was a human chain stretching all the way to the hammerhead on both sides of the taxiway. They had come to watch us go fight, not knowing if we'd be coming home. And as we passed, the last bomber to taxi, whole groups of them came to attention and gave us a salute. This was repeated until we were on the runway, and it made me realise that they were all in for as sleepless a night as we were. It was the best expression of human dignity I've ever seen, or ever expect to see.

'The cruise up to the peninsula was uneventful. We lost our primary No 2 to a malfunctioning electronic jamming suite – he elected to RTB, and a spare filled in. We completed our chaff, flare and arming checks and proceeded to our Start Descent point. The radios were noisy as all the evening's "players" began checking in – adding to the radio chatter, a ruse had been cooked up about a downed aircraft to mask the force building just south of the border. The Iraqis were being led to believe that we were all searching for a downed aeroplane in Saudi.

'Just as we started our descent, the fill-in No 2 declared that his radar director for his tail guns had failed, and he dropped out to RTB. We were left with only two aircraft, and rather than a razzle-dazzle multi-axis attack, we were down to an extended single axis delivery. Just enough time for the AAA gunners to wake up.

'We killed the lights and dropped below radar, pushed it up, calibrated our terrain avoidance radar set, then turned it to STANDBY to minimise emissions. This was to be a night, seat-of-the-pants sortie. Upstairs at the pilots' station, we wore Night Vision Goggles, and downstairs the navigators monitored the Low Light TV and IR cameras. The fight was on! Crossing the border, we saw a truck with dimmed headlights heading south. Hoping it hadn't noticed us, we arced around it and went "in country". We saw all kinds of anti-aircraft fire in front of us, but never having been shot at before, we did not stop to think that it was well clear. In point of fact, the fire was coming from the Basra area, and was most likely greeting the first wave of guys in on Talil airfield. Our turn would come soon enough. We elected to turn away from the perceived threat and lean towards the target a little early. Since No 2 had fallen out, we could afford to close on Lead a little.

'Things were quiet right up to the Initial Point of the bomb run, a scant five minutes later. As Lead passed over the target and dropped his weapons, a lone AAA gun spat at him. We knew there were four more gun emplacements at the target, and we were 90 seconds in trail. Forty seconds later, the world in front of us opened up, with tracers galore from multiple points. Still four miles out from the target, on the deck, we began jinking to confound anyone trying to get a bead on us. The tracers and muzzle flashes were intense enough to turn night into day, and I took off my goggles.

'The Low Light TV camera went to standby – the light had tripped a feature designed to

Groundcrew service the four 0.50-in machine guns in the remotely controlled tail turret of a B-52G during *Desert Storm*. Soon after the war, the surviving 'Buffs' were 'Bobbited', losing their tail turrets and their gunners (*Andy Bloom*)

Tanker crews are fond of pointing out that 'No-one kicks ass without tanker gas!', and this was particularly the case for the Diego Garcia 'Buffs', which flew further than any other B-52 detachments to reach their targets, excepting the one-way sorties mounted from Wurtsmith and the *Secret Squirrel* mission from Barksdale (*Andy Bloom*)

protect the camera from damage when flying into direct sunlight. I started to lower my seat, then elected not to – the thin aircraft skin would afford little protection from the volley of shells. The aircraft shuddered as the weapons fell off, and then we were through the curtain, unscathed except for a nagging "Master Caution" light that had illuminated. Although this is a normal occurrence when the bomb-bay doors are closed, we momentarily entertained the notion of Battle Damage. But upon closer examination of the aircraft systems, we realised that we were okay, but not out of the woods yet.

'Our target area egress was supposed to be a wide, sweeping left turn to a rejoin with us as Lead on the way home. The turn went okay, but the rejoin part was below standard – an Iraqi army division messed things up. We were both going as fast as the "BUFF" could go, and in this case, faster than was prudent, and we couldn't catch up. Lead, now in trail as No 2, told us later that several shoulder-launched IR SAMs were fired at us on the way out, but we were ignorant of it at the time. What had got our attention was a radar lock-on from a ZSU-23-4 – the modern-day equivalent of a flakpanzer. Our EWO, Capt Glenn Traver, saved us with jamming and timely chaff. The ZSU fired, but only hit floating tinsel foil.

'They must have lost us at this time, because the next thing the Iraqis did was to launch heavy artillery shells fitted with magnesium illuminators – shells that glow for a long time while the lit charge slowly descends via parachute. I felt like Lady Godiva as the light cast a shadow of the aeroplane on the ground below, naked for all to see. We must have been out of range, or they never reacquired us, because we made the border uneventfully. We slowed, got our lights on and effected a rejoin, then climbed up into a cloud deck that had moved in off the Gulf.

'The next thing we knew, strange lights were all around us in the haze – F-14 Tomcats from a nearby carrier were making sure Iraqi fighters weren't trying to sneak out into the Gulf intermixed with us. This close checking was known as delousing. As they completed their inspection and moved off to wait for their next border-crossers, we collectively breathed a sigh of relief. We were home safe and sound, and the "friendlies" had caught us. Now all we had to do was fly back to Diego.

'As the night progressed, messages began to filter back to the island that rather than 30 per cent casualties, we had zero. Everyone was coming home, and the overall first night of the air campaign had dealt the Iraqis a blow from which they would never recover. We had done well. One of the bombers even got a "ground kill" credit, as an IrAF fighter taxiing out to intercept us blew up as it taxied over a Gator mine at one of the airfields.

'We were the first bomber to land of all those launched from Diego that night. When we landed, the same throng of people lined the taxiways to greet the returning bombers. We were spirited off the jet – hands appeared from nowhere to grab our gear and put it on the crew bus. Bob Fournier was lifted up to stencil a bomb on the side of the aircraft, and we were welcomed with much jubilation. We all felt about a mile tall.

'I flew several missions after that one – each is notable in its own way. Some nights the flak was so intense I felt I could have walked on it. Other nights, I just wanted to rain bombs down on the enemy, like the night Navy Lt Jeffrey Zaun appeared beaten on Iraqi TV. None, however, can compare to that first mission because of the way it changed us.'

Whatever the reason, Brig Gen 'Buster' Glosson soon ordered that all coalition aircraft should observe a minimum attack level of 12,000 ft. Once pulled from low-level attacks, the B-52s flew higher still, bombing from 32,000 to 37,000 ft. While it did probably improve overall survivability, the change in tactics also resulted in much reduced accuracy with unguided weapons, since at these heights even large targets like aircraft hangars were often too small to recognise and identify. When dropping from these altitudes, the B-52G's bombs usually hit within a few hundred feet of the target. That was no match for the accuracy of a laser-guided bomb, but it was ideal for use against large-area targets.

At the start of the war, the B-52Gs often had dedicated F-15 escorts, although from the halfway point of aerial campaign onwards, they relied on 'area' Combat Air Patrols, which meant that there would be fighters airborne, but not dedicated to protecting the bombers specifically. Similarly, while the B-52Gs initially operated with dedicated F-4Gs for SAM suppression, these aircraft were so heavily tasked that they soon had to rely on 'area' SEAD (Suppression of Enemy Air Defense) on some missions and no SEAD support at all on others.

Throughout *Desert Storm*, the Diego Garcia-based B-52Gs relied heavily on tanker support. With missions typically lasting about 17 hours from take-off to landing, the aircraft topped off their tanks from Diego-based tankers about an hour after take-off, and then rendezvoused with KC-135 tankers from Oman or Bahrain four hour later, refuelling twice before crossing the Saudi border into Iraq or Kuwait.

The B-52s also operated hand-in-hand with E-3 AWACS platforms, checking in with a 'strike controller' as they got close to the border to be briefed on the tactical situation, threats and any target changes. The latter became the norm, with reconnaissance assets locating a suitable target in Kuwait or Iraq and transmitting its coordinates to an E-3 while the cell of B-52s were still one hour or more away. The AWACS aircraft would then forward new target information to the bomber via coded message.

The B-52s were heavily used against the Iraqi Republican Guard and Iraqi Army in the field, flying missions against enemy troops around the clock to demoralise them and deny them any rest. For softer targets, the B-52Gs used the CBU-58 and CBU-52 cluster bombs, which were used to devastating effect to thin out Iraqi troop strength.

The B-52Gs often had a tight target timing window in order to avoid damaging friendly aircraft. 'When all our bombs go off, shrapnel fills the air up to 2000 ft high, 2000 ft wide and a half-mile long. Any aeroplane flying through that would be shot down', Clonts explained.

B-52Gs also flew interdiction missions, often at night, against railroad yards, ammunition factories, storage areas, fuel depots, industrial sites and airfields, using 750-lb M117 bombs, 500-lb Mk 82s and CBU-87s. B-52s were also active in the campaign to suppress Iraq's defences, using CBUs against radar and SAM sites. Diego Garcia's B-52s also joined the 'great Scud hunt', working alongside F-15Es to find and destroy missile launchers using CBU-87 anti-tank cluster bombs.

Although some B-52 missions were little more than 'milk runs', others were packed with danger, coming under AAA and SAM fire. On the night of 20 January 1991, for example, Capt Allan G Hagelthorn flew a mission which resulted in his being awarded the Distinguished Flying Cross.

Flying his first combat sortie as part of a six-ship strike package targeted against a radio transmitting facility just north of Baghdad, Hagelthorn's jet (which had an inoperative tail warning receiver and only one jamming transmitter) came under heavy SAM fire, but Hagelthorn manoeuvred the aircraft left and right of track throughout the bomb run to degrade the missile radars that were tracking him. Remaining committed to the attack run, he pulled the B-52 into a 50-degree banked breaking turn only after the navigator called 'Bombs away, break right pilot!'

Subsequent bomb damage assessment of the target showed that the mission had been successful. Capt Hagelthorn's bombs were perfectly spaced the length of the target, and the damage caused was so heavy and precise that the facility never transmitted again. Col Burke said later that, 'Capt Hagelthorn and his crew performed in an absolutely flawless manner, countering numerous enemy attacks despite numerous defensive equipment failures, and delivered their bombs on target.'

On 3 February the 4300th BW(P) suffered the only 'Buff' aircrew casualties of the war when B-52G 59-2593 experienced a catastrophic electrical system failure while returning to Diego Garcia. Flying at 2000 ft, and just 12 miles from landing, the bomber experienced total electrical failure and all eight engines lost power. Improper fuel management by the crew caused five engines to flame out, and the aircraft began to descend. In an increasingly rapid descent, the crew realised that the B-52 could not recover. Three crewmen ejected safely before the jet crashed into the Indian Ocean, but the remaining three ejected too late and were killed.

1708th BW(P)'s WAR

B-52s based at Jeddah flew more than half of the total wartime Stratofortress missions (841 of 1625 sorties). Jeddah's 'Buffs' also dropped more munitions than the rest of the B-52 wings combined (36,580 of the 72,289 bombs dropped by B-52Gs). Even more amazingly, the Jeddah-based 1708th BW(P) was responsible for 20 per cent of *all* bombs dropped during the war by Coalition aircraft.

Jeddah's B-52Gs dropped a total of 25,750,000 lbs (gross) of bombs, with 11,742,000 lbs (net) of explosive weight. These comprised 22,532 M117s, 8261 Mk 82s, 2122 CBU-52s, 3278 CBU-58s and 387 CBU-71/87/89s. The 500-lb Mk 82s were expended early in the campaign, forcing a reliance on the older M117 750-lb weapons. The fleet of aircraft averaged 24 sorties per day, generating 29 sorties on one day and achieving a 99.6 per cent drop rate.

As previously mentioned, during *Desert Shield*, the Saudi government had grave reservations about the B-52, and would not initially allow 'Buff' crews to train in its airspace, let alone actually use its bases. It was clear, however, that the latter restriction would be dropped as soon as the war began, and plans were put in place to station a wing of B-52Gs at King Abdul Aziz International Airport, also known as Jeddah New.

Although no aircraft were deployed, a site survey was conducted between 16 and 26 October 1990, and this found that Jeddah New was well suited 'for B-52G sustainability', and the base was approved for 'Buff' operations on 28 October. Before the B-52 detachment began, seven KC-135 crews formed the 920th AREFS(P) at Jeddah. From 9 November, a six-man ops planning team was maintained at Jeddah, its members being rotated every two to three weeks to give the maximum number of people early experience of in-theatre requirements, and enabling the planning set-up to be massively expanded when required.

On 20 December, a single B-52G from Diego Garcia deployed to Jeddah for taxi and parking tests, returning home later that same day. The Saudi government finally agreed to the deployment of a full B-52 wing two weeks before the war began. The first two 'Buff' crews deployed to Jeddah (aboard incoming KC-135s) on 3 January 1991, and another arrived aboard a KC-10 on 12 January 1991.

Desert Storm began at 0300 hrs (Baghdad time) on 17 January 1991 (1900 hrs EST on 16 January) when targets in Iraq were hit by Coalition aircraft and cruise missiles.

Six of the 18 B-52Gs launched from Diego Garcia from 2009 hrs Baghdad time on 16 January flew

A mission involving just two cells of B-52s would require a substantial briefing room, with six crews of six. Here, six of the 1708th BW(P)'s B-52 crews brief for their next mission (*Andy Bloom*)

on to Jeddah after attacking their targets. The 1708th BW(P) would soon receive further aircraft despatched all the way from Wurtsmith AFB.

Twelve B-52Gs launched from the Michigan base in the early hours of 18 January 1991, flying what would become the longest employ–deploy strike mission in history, up to this time.

The aircraft consisted of seven from the 379th BW, three from the 93rd and two from the 42nd. And although the aircraft were drawn from a number of units, all were flown by crews from the 524th BS/379th BW, and these carried a total of 288 CBU-87 cluster bombs and 135 M117 general purpose bombs.

The formation consisted of three cells of four B-52s, with a 'spare' aircraft in each cell. The first wave comprised 58-0173 *Let's Make A Deal* of the 379th BW (flown by Crew S-30 and captained by Capt Reed Estrada), 58-0218, borrowed from the 42nd BW (flown by Crew R-25 and captained by Capt Russ Bennet), and 59-2570 *Ole Baldy* from the 93rd BW (flown by Crew R-17 and captained by Capt Gary Konnert). Capt Steve Lees and Crew E-23 flew 59-2591 as the air spare. This 379th BW aircraft later joined the 801st BW(P) at Moron.

The second wave was led by 58-0194 *Buffasaurus* of the 379th BW (flown by Crew S-20, captained by Capt Berry Sebring), accompanied by 58-0203 of the 93rd BW (flown by Crew E-19, captained by Capt Randy Long) and 57-6492 *Old Crow Express* of the 379th BW (flown by Crew R-14, captained by Capt Steve Heflin). The spare was 57-6474 *Lone Wolf* of the 379th BW, which later joined the 801st BW(P).

The third wave was led by 58-0175 *Viper* of the 379th BW (flown by Crew S-10, captained by

B-52Gs of the 1708th BW dispersed at Jeddah during *Desert Storm*. The base was closer to the B-52s' targets than any of the other airfields used by the type during *Desert Storm* (*Andy Bloom*)

The 'Triangle K' marking of the 379th BG seen on the tail of 58-0173 *Let's Make A Deal*. Directly taken from the unit's World War 2-era marking, this insignia was used by arguably the most important and hard-worked of all the B-52 wings to see action in *Desert Storm* (*Andy Bloom*)

Let's Make A Deal (58-0173) led the first wave in the attack mounted from Wurtsmith AFB, and went on to complete 42 missions, totalling 190.6 combat hours. The aircraft's nose art showed *Donald Duck*, in a sailor's suit, about to throw a fizzing bomb and shaking his fist (*Andy Bloom*)

58-0218 of the 42nd BW shows off its characteristic 'wrinkled' fuselage sides, a function of the need to pressurise the fuselage. This aircraft flew 28 sorties from Jeddah before transferring to Moron (*Andy Bloom*)

B-52G 58-0194 *Buffasaurus* led the second cell on the historic mission from Wurtsmith on 18 January 1991, being flown by Capt Berry Sebring and Crew S-20. It went on to log 208.2 combat flying hours during the course of 46 missions (*Andy Bloom*)

Capt Seth Junkins). The remaining aircraft in the cell were 58-0159 *Alley Oops Bold Assault* of the 379th BW (flown by Crew R-15, captained by Capt Bill Borras), 58-0192 of the 42nd BW (flown by Crew R-34, captained by Capt Mark Batway) and 59-2598 of the 93rd BW (flown by Crew S-02, captained by Capt John McDonough).

About five hours into the mission, the air spares in the first and second cells turned back to Wurtsmith, although the third cell continued on as a four-aircraft formation.

Andy Bloom was the navigator on the lead aircraft in the first cell, and he described the mission as follows:

'My crew and I entered the war on Day 2. We flew 58-0173 *Let's Make A Deal* as the lead ship out of Wurtsmith. We launched from our base at about 0400 hrs on 18 January 1991. We were the Lead "Buff" in the first formation out of a total of ten B-52Gs launched from Wurtsmith on that day. Our first air refuelling took place off the east coast, outbound from the United States. There was a spare jet that flew in our formation, and it would take on any position if one of the primary jets broke, or might have had problems delivering its weapons. If everyone was okay, then the spare would head back to Wurtsmith. Our second air refuelling took place over the Straits of Gibraltar.

'The mission was going smoothly until we hit the Egyptian coast. We had lost radio contact with the Italian Air Traffic Control Centre and failed to gain contact with anyone until midway across Egypt. Every

B-52G 57-6492 *Old Crow Express* was another ALCM carrier from the 379th BW at Wurtsmith AFB sent to war, the bomber flying as the third aircraft in the second cell during the famous 18 January 1991 mission. Flown then by Capt Steve Heflin and Crew R-14, 57-6492 wore a cartoon crow, in 1940s flying kit (and spats), leaning on a bomb on its nose, together with a mission log featuring 54 bombs – the 50th bomb in the log was marked in red. Having not got to drop its bombs on the 18 January mission, 57-6492 flew all 54 of its missions from Jeddah. It had amassed 233.1 combat hours by war's end (*Andy Bloom*)

B-52G 58-0175 was also an ALCM carrier from the 379th BW at Wurtsmith, the bomber being fitted with long pylons, seen here carrying CBUs. *Viper* led the third cell from Wurtsmith on 18 January 1991, flown by Capt Seth Junkins' S-10 crew. The aircraft flew 47 missions from Jeddah, logging 215.8 combat flying hours (*Andy Bloom*)

Egyptian piece of defensive equipment came up and "locked" onto us. A friendly voice called us on guard and established radio contact with us. After tap dancing around for several minutes, the US Navy scrambled a pair of F/A-18s to establish visual contact and escort us across the Red Sea.

'By now we were running five minutes late, and all three aircraft were low on fuel. We were in contact with the Coalition headquarters in Saudi Arabia, and they were trying to get us another air refuelling, either prior to our targets or after our bomb runs.

'Anyway, our worst nightmare was about to come true. We were heading into battle and unable to contact our AWACS aircraft! Just prior to taking off, we had received a communications log with appropriate frequencies for the southern zone. Unfortunately, we were in the northern zone! Finally, we were able to establish contact with the AWACS, and we told them of our situation. Then we heard the code words for return-to-base (RTB) and proceeded accordingly. Next, they told us the mission was back on, so we made another 180-degree turn and headed towards our target.

'In the meantime, there was a new Zulu time change. After crossing the Iraqi border, and 20 minutes from the target, the AWACS gave us another code word. Again, we didn't have the codes for the new Zulu day! Basically, AWACS was telling us to RTB because we had lost our support package – i.e.

Maj Andy Bloom, who supplied many of the photographs used in this book, poses beside a load of CBU-58 cluster bombs under the wing of his crew's aircraft, 58-0173 *Let's Make A Deal* (*Andy Bloom*)

Groundcrew work on the wing of 58-0253, a former 42nd BW aircraft which transferred from Diego Garcia to Jeddah on 17 January, and which went on to fly 52 missions, totalling 214.6 flying hours. The way in which the name *LORING* followed the line of the rudder is clearly shown, as is the moose's head and Maine badge used as unit markings by the 42nd BW (*Andy Bloom*)

fighter protection and SAM suppression assets. As we were heading south for our base, we picked up another air refuelling over Saudi Arabia. One aircraft had 15,000 lbs of gas before plugging into the tanker. In the bomber world, he had about 30 minutes of flying time remaining, and our base was over 45 minutes away! After 18.5 hours in the air, we landed at our forward operating area (FOL) in Saudi Arabia to become part of the 1708th BW(P)/1701st SW(P).'

In the event, only the four B-52s in Cell 3 dropped bombs in Iraq. Cell 1 was recalled by an E-3 Sentry AWACS, as described by Andy Bloom, while Cell 3 ran low on fuel when it was forced to bypass a storm. All ten aircraft recovered in Saudi Arabia, where they joined the 1708th BW(P). The ten Wurtsmith aircraft and crews, and six aircraft and crews from Diego Garcia, were later augmented by a 2nd BW and three 416th BW aircraft from Moron, and by a number of new crews.

During the first few days of the war, B-52Gs made a number of daring low-level attacks, many of them against heavily defended enemy airfields. As the air campaign progressed, however, they were increasingly assigned to medium-level 'carpet bombing' sorties against the Republican Guard, minefields and storage areas. When Gen Norman Schwarzkopf decreed that the Republican Guard should be hit every three hours, the B-52G force found these missions taking up about 85 per cent of its efforts.

Only about 36 low-level sorties were flown, one of them by Crew E-13, which included Capts Tony Monetti (co-pilot) and Jonny Iverson (EWO), who together flew 17 missions from Diego Garcia and Jeddah. They told their story to aviation author Tony Cassanova, who kindly allowed it to be included in this chapter. Captain Monetti remembered:

'Before our first mission, we became familiar with the threats by way of the Intel folks and crews who had flown on Nights One and Two. The main threat seemed to be AAA. The reason we were going low level was the air-to-air threat. We knew that they had a very significant air element, so consequently the main threat against the "Flying Barn", as we call the B-52, was air-to-air. On the evening of our first mission – on 18 January, which was Night Three of the war – ten aircraft were readied, of which two were spares. The eight primary bombers were split into two cells of four. Our cell's target was an oil refinery south of Baghdad, near As Samawah. Our aircraft was No 4, and along with No 3, we were going to attack the storage tank farm, while Lead and No 2 took out the control facility.

'We soon descended to low level over Saudi and discovered the entire region was fogged in. We had envisioned a 200-ft ingress altitude, but we were at 400 ft because the jet's terrain avoidance set wasn't working – the radar beam was skipping off the sand. In addition, the NVGs we were wearing were ineffective due to fog.

'The plan for our four-ship cell was to split into two-ship elements

and prosecute a multi-axis attack on the target so as to confuse the enemy. The timing was very close, so it was critical that we released our weapons on time and on the proper axis of attack, otherwise the cell might "frag" itself. When the lead ship of our element dropped out with radar problems, we were directed to make up Lead's time, meaning a 100 per cent power setting. We also had to cut a few corners, which made it very challenging for the navigation team. The only thing we were flying off was the radar altimeter, which was crazy. As soon as we'd see it get a little low, we'd pull up. I even said to the AC (Aircraft Commander), "The regs say we don't go." He replied, "The regs don't apply in combat."

'The bomb run was very short, and began with a right turn roll-in IP. Because of a tall tower in the middle of our attack axis, we couldn't execute less than 30 degrees of bank in the final turn from the roll-in IP, but if we exceeded this the radar altimeter would break lock and we'd be flying off nothing but the regular pressure altimeter. To get us on the proper axis, the Nav said, "I need you to come right and give me 45 degrees of bank." There was a tense exchange between the pilot and Nav at this point, one trying to save the bomb run while the other tried to save the aircraft. Both were right. We had corrected too far right of track.

'We were forced to abort our attack, and the navigators loaded the coordinates for the secondary target. Then the AC of the cell came over the radio to say we could return to the target, as they had encountered no threats. The Iraqis had just had over 100 bombs dropped on their heads, so I was sure they were up now. The AWACS came back and replied, "If you guys are up for it, go ahead!" So we did a 180-degree turn and a 19-minute "racetrack", just like in the movie *Memphis Belle*. As we came in with eight seconds to go, the shit hit the fan. I remember seeing red tracers coming at us from the right, and within seconds of that, the AC yelled, "I've got AAA at

This view of a conventional G-model taking off shows the jet's large flaps to advantage, while the chaff/flare dispenser embedded in the port tailplane can also be discerned (*Andy Bloom*)

The way in which the Strategic Camouflage 'wrapped' over the undersurface of the B-52G is clearly apparent in this view of a 1708th BW(P) aircraft. The nearest jet is a CMI (Cruise Missile Integrated) machine, and has the longer underwing pylons, while the conventional ICSMS aircraft behind uses the shorter underwing pylon design (*Andy Bloom*)

58-0192 is seen from the cockpit of another 1708th BW(P) aircraft en route to the target. Originally from the 42nd BW at Loring AFB, 58-0192 flew 49 missions (216 hours), starting with the historic raid launched from Wurtsmith. The aircraft was No 3 in the third cell, and was flown by Capt Mark Batway and Crew R-34. Later named *East Coast Outlaw*, the B-52 ended the war adorned with a 53-bomb mission tally, every tenth weapon applied in red (*Andy Bloom*)

B-52G 57-6501 *Ragin Red* came from the 416th BW at Griffiss AFB, and flew six missions (95.2 hours) from Moron before moving to Jeddah, where it flew ten more, totalling 44 hours. The aircraft's nose art featured a muscular red bull stomping on a red star. The bomb log consisted of a black camel and five black bombs, with ten white bombs added at Jeddah (*Andy Bloom*)

nine o'clock!" All you could see were these red things coming through the fog. I thought for sure we were taking hits. It was now "4, 3, 2, 1 . . . release". I had never dropped 51 750-lb bombs in my life, and during the release the aircraft shook pretty violently as if we were driving over a rough road.'

In the bowels of the 'Buff', the EWO, Capt Iverson was similarly concerned:

'I actually thought we were taking hits! I just looked at the gunner as if to say, "God, this is it!" We both reached for our ejection handles, then we shared a seemingly psychic experience when we simultaneously realised it was the M117s coming off the jet.'

Capt Monetti continues his recollection of the mission:

'As we continued through the AAA, I was still wearing my goggles, and the fog was now starting to burn off due to the excessive heat from the fires. I could now see the tanks ahead of our aircraft as our weapons began going off behind us. Suddenly, it was like a nuclear detonation! I'll never forget this – the fog lit up like a bright light, and the AC and I were temporarily blinded. About five seconds later the "E-Dub" (EWO) called out, "Pilot. SAM – hunker!"

'The way we operated the "BUFF" at low level is that one guy flew it while the other controlled the throttles. I was the "speed" guy while the AC was the "left-right-up-and-down" guy. The AC pushed the nose down and the countermeasures worked as the missile locked onto either our chaff or flares. And this is the point where we almost hit the ground. I saw my radar altimeter start to bottom out, so I grabbed the yoke, wrapped both arms around it and pulled it back. I thought for sure we were going to hit when the altimeter locked on at 50 ft.

'People facing near death have said that time slows down, and it did, but during this period I didn't think about my wife and children. I thought about what a priest had said to me earlier that evening – God

would never abandon me. So, I was at peace. However every one was screaming out, "Climb, climb!" We did start to climb, and as the AC looked over at me, I could see there were beads of sweat pouring off his face, and he was as white as a ghost! I grabbed him by the arm and asked if he was all right. He replied that he couldn't let go of the yoke – he had a death grip on it.

'Upon returning home, I spoke to a few Boeing engineers regarding our ordeal of almost impacting the ground, and they were convinced that the large underwing surface and ground effect cushioned the aircraft that night. This, plus the right angle of attack, saved our lives. We obviously pulled up at just the right time. Then the AAA started up again.'

Capt Iverson recalled that:

'We managed to re-enter Saudi airspace in search of a tanker, but our problems were not over. It was freezing in the back of the cabin, so I asked Tony to turn up the heat. He responded to the whole crew with, "Hey, we've got a fire light!" That statement quickly re-tightened our sphincters, and we started a whole new pain-in-the-ass adventure on this sortie from hell.'

Capt. Monetti explained that:

'As we were exiting Iraq and climbing out of low level, I started to turn on the instrument lighting, and I immediately got the fire warning light on engine number five, so we shut it down, but the light stayed on. I figured it was because we had taken hits, so as a precaution we shut down the adjacent engine.'

Monetti passed an emergency message to the AWACS via another member of the B-52 element, but he was not to know that the E-3 had already gone off duty. The crew then had to find their way to Jeddah, unable at first to find its coordinates, as they did not know the full title of the base (King Abdul Aziz Airport). They were guided by a Saudi controller who spoke very little English, and who warned them not to overfly Mecca or they would be shot down. Finally, the SAC Runway Supervisory Officer at Jeddah talked them in.

Surprisingly despite the damage caused to their target, none of the crew ever received a commendation for this mission.

The 1708th BW(P) had a strength of 16 Primary Aircraft Authorised, although official figures do not tally, since they included five ALCM jets from the 379th and three from the 416th BWs, five '777s' from the 93rd and four from the 42nd. A total of 20 B-52Gs were actually deployed (not simultaneously) to Jeddah – eight from the 42nd, five from the 379th, three each from the 93rd and 416th and a solitary jet from the 2nd.

B-52G 58-0164 *SAC Time* joined the 1708th BW(P) from Moron, the aircraft having flown six sorties from Spain (totalling 77.8 hours). It went on to complete 26 more (119.3 hours) from Jeddah. The B-52 originally came from the 416th BW at Griffiss AFB (*Andy Bloom*)

When fully fuelled, a B-52's outrigger undercarriage touches the ground. Here, a bombed and fuelled up 1708th BW(P) 'Buff' waits for its crew (*Andy Bloom*)

Air and ground crews were similarly drawn from throughout the B-52 force, with the 29 load crews including personnel from units operating the B-52H (the load crews came from the 2nd, 5th, 7th, 42nd, 92nd, 93rd, 97th, 379th, 410th and 416th MMS).

Scott Moore was assigned to the 1708 BW(P) as a staff instructor pilot from the 416th BW:

'At Jeddah, I believe the wing staff and a majority of the crews were from Wurtsmith, but we had approximately three crews from Griffiss. It was very hard for a non-Wurtsmith guy to get added to a mission. I spent most of my time there as an SOF, pre-flighting aeroplanes, helping mission-plan and trying to get on a mission.'

While Scott Moore did not fly a *Desert Storm* mission, Wurtsmith-based navigator Andy Bloom managed to play a very active part:

'Of the 24 combat missions I flew over Iraq and Kuwait, about three of these sorties were pretty hairy. The first memorable incident occurred during our second mission, when our target was Republican Guard forces dug in along the Iraqi/Kuwaiti border. We were No 3 in a three-ship formation of B-52Gs. We had just released our weapons – M117s – and made the post target turn heading for our base. The co-pilot was watching a friendly fighter off our right wing when, all of a sudden, the pilot announced SAMs, and began manoeuvring to avoid them. The EWO called "I've got no missile guidance!", meaning the missiles were launched unguided at us.

'In the meantime, the rest of us were bracing for impact at any moment because we couldn't see outside the aircraft, and therefore did not know how far away the missiles were from us. We spent the next two minutes, what seemed an eternity, manoeuvring until we were out of the threat zone. Apparently, four missiles were shot at us with no impact and, according to the pilot, they were about four miles from us.

'The second incident was during a daytime raid on a weapon storage facility south-west of Basra. Our planning staff had worked out a support package with the US Navy and Marines, because they were working in the same area as our mission. After checking in with AWACS about our package, the Navy's response was, "I'm not working them". With comments like those, we knew something was wrong! About 15 minutes from the bomb run, we heard the following warning from a US

Armourers load 750-lb M117 bombs under the wing of 58-0173 *Let's Make A Deal*. The 'Buff's' ability to carry very large bombloads imposed a major strain on the supply chain (*Andy Bloom*)

Navy/Marine F/A-18 Hornet – "Aircraft at such and such position, identify yourself!" AWACS began to inform the pilot that we were "friendly chicks, so leave them alone". This went back and forth for about four minutes. After being spooked, the Hornet pilot got a "lock on" and asked permission to fire his missiles! Finally, somebody informed our friend that we were B-52s at such and such altitude, position, and airspeed. So much for communications security, and not letting the Iraqis know our position!

Three 1708th BW(P) B-52s taxi out at the start of yet another mission. The lead jet is an ICSMS aircraft from the 42nd BW (*Andy Bloom*)

Andy Bloom and his crew pose together at Jeddah prior to flying a *Desert Storm* mission. The aircraft in the background is 58-0159, which ended the war with a mission tally featuring 46 white bombs. Its nose art consisted of a caveman wielding a stone club and throwing a bomb, as well as the unusual name *Alley Oops Bold Assault*. The aircraft flew on the first historic raid launched from Wurtsmith, flown by Capt Bill Borras and Crew R-15, and then went on to complete 46 missions and 205.9 combat flying hours from Jeddah (*Andy Bloom*)

This appeared to calm our Navy/Marine buddy down, but not very much. We later learned the AWACS replayed the tape recordings, got his call-sign, and tracked him down. We hoped his commanding officer had a good talk with him!

'The third event was a night raid on an oil refinery and petroleum storage facility. This mission called for two formations of three B-52Gs, with five minutes' separation between formations. The plan called for a multi-axis attack to get the maximum weapons coverage across the target, without hitting the civilian community, and their mosque. Aircraft Nos 1, 2, 4 and 5 had a west-to-east axis, and Nos 3 and 6 had a south-west to north-east axis. This called for a different routing for Nos 3 and 6 – we were No 3 aircraft in this formation. It was a good plan, but suffered from one problem. Because of the routing, Nos 3 (us) and 6 ended up gaining time, and thus changing formation lead over the target! This would not have been so bad if there was prior coordination, but there wasn't any.

'Our first indication that a problem existed was coming up to the target. I was watching the target in the FLIR camera, and I didn't see the lead jet's weapons detonating within the target area. After our weapons release, we started to look for the other aircraft when the gunner called out, "I've got five aircraft behind us." After some time, we determined those aircraft were the rest of the formation. We began to realise what could have happened if our timing was a little different. Since we stacked up in altitude during formation flights, we were in the higher position, and our weapons dropped down through the other aircraft's altitude! We could have lost several aircraft due to this plan, and the route we flew.

'There were some interesting phrases that we came up with while over there. When a mission called for bombing the minefields along the Kuwaiti and Saudi border, it was a "make a run for the border" or "Taco Bell run" [named after a TV commercial for Taco Bell]. This was because our bomb release line – a point in-flight where the bombs needed to be released to hit their target – was in Saudi Arabia, and our post-target turn kept our jets within country as well. We had the "Baghdad Express" name for those missions going up to Baghdad.'

Despite the various dramas, no Jeddah B-52Gs were lost to enemy action, although several were damaged. One B-52G was damaged by a hit from an unknown type of missile, but was able to make it home safely. Another lost two engines as a result of a near-miss by a SA-3 SAM, and B-52 58-0253 was damaged by shrapnel from exploding AAA fire. The latter was being flown by Col Kenneth Boykin, CO of the 1708th BW(P) at the time, as Senior Master Sergeant Mike Jones later recalled:

'Jeddah's very long runway had a taxiway that completely surrounded the active runway. This allowed us to perform what I call a round robin-type launch and recovery operation. The "Buffs" would land and go into the overrun area, then taxi left and head back in the opposite direction. They would stop in an area where a team would run chemical detection tapes across the airframe. They would then continue down the taxiway to Pits 3 and 4, where they were gassed up ready for the next mission. When we finished gassing these "Buffs", one of us would ride in the co-pilot's seat as a pilot or co-pilot taxied it down to the end of the runway and parked it in the main maintenance area near the hangers. There, the bombs would be loaded and the aircraft prepared for its next mission.

'Pit 3 was designated as where all in-flight emergencies would land. As I marshalled 58-0253 in, I noticed that fuel was literally streaming out of every tank except the forward area of the aircraft. The jet stopped and the crew performed an emergency egress. The damage was tremendous. I personally counted at least 100 holes in the aircraft. The left external tank on this aircraft was peeled back from the rear like a banana (see the photograph on page 9). The left external tank on a "Buff" holds 4400 lbs of gas. The left and right outboard tanks were leaking, along with the Nos 1, 2, 3 and 4 mains. Looking at the aft body tank, you could actually see daylight through the fuselage. Inside the 47 section there was fuel everywhere, and I picked up numerous pieces of shrapnel. These ranged in size from small pebbles through to a man's fist. I gave the largest to Col Kenneth Boykin, who happened to be flying the aircraft that day. The navigator's lower ejection hatch also had a large hole in it where a piece of metal had entered and lodged in his seat.

'Our "Buffs" were flying three-ship formations, and '0253 was in the rear position when an SA-6 exploded near to the aircraft. I think the jet was flying an evasive manoeuvre at the time, as some of the shrapnel went in sideways. We drained all the fuel out of the aircraft and towed it down to where the Aircraft Battle Damage Repair team could patch the holes and get it back home.'

Although attrition was negligible, the pace of operations did mean that many of the deployed B-52Gs were 'running out of hours' by mid-

B-52G 58-0164 *SAC Time* was a CMI jet from the 416th BW at Griffiss, and was fitted with the long Hound Dog-type pylon. The aircraft flew six missions (77.8 hours) from Moron, before transferring to Jeddah, where it completed 26 more (119.3 hours). The B-52's bomb-log began with a palm tree, a camel and seven bombs in black, and new bombs (in white) were added low on the nose at Jeddah (*Andy Bloom*)

Trailing thick black smoke, this conventional B-52G was photographed shortly after taking off from Jeddah. Its short bomb pylons are clearly evident (*Andy Bloom*)

By contrast, ALCM-modified 58-0194 (the much illustrated *Buffasaurus*) shows off its longer Hound Dog-type underwing pylons and 'faired' wingroots as it takes off from the same runway (*Andy Bloom*)

February, and would need to be rotated home for major maintenance. With more than half of the USAF's B-52Gs deployed, replacing the aircraft would clearly be difficult. Finding replacement aircrew was less of a problem, as a pilot who served with the 1708th BW(P) explained:

'While I was at Jeddah, I ran into at least one crew who were dual-qualified in both the G- and H-model B-52, and I was led to understand that there were H-model crews in the B-52G pipeline at Castle who were being prepped to come in and relieve the crews in-theatre. However, the short duration of the war precluded any H-model crews from actually getting into combat, as far as I am aware.'

Eventually, it was decided that the best solution would be to send B-52Hs, and their crews, and plans to launch a nine-jet strike from Carswell, landing at Jeddah, were well advanced when the war ended.

The sudden end to the war also removed any possibility of using the AGM-142A 'Have Nap' stand-off guided weapon. The AGM-142A Raptor was a derivative of the Israeli Rafael Popeye, jointly developed with Lockheed Martin. The weapon was a precision-guided, air-to-ground missile designed for use against high-value ground targets including missile sites, bridges, ships and bunkers. The AGM-142 used inertial mid-course guidance, then employed TV or imaging IR (IIR) terminal guidance, depending on the sensor installed in the particular version of the missile The AGM-142A uses a blast fragmentation warhead and TV guidance, the AGM-142B employs blast fragmentation and IIR, the AGM-142C has a penetrator and TV, and the AGM-142D uses a penetrator and IIR.

The missile was controlled by the radar navigator aboard the B-52G using a small joystick and an IR or TV display. The B-52G could carry four AGM-142s on each of its underwing pylons (or three plus a datalink pod), each with a 1000-lb blast fragmentation or penetrator warhead.

Scott Moore recalled 'seeing AGM-142s in crates at Jeddah when I gave a tour to a group of Saudi officers. They were not used in combat as far as I am aware. I was told that the political sensitivities of using what was essentially an Israeli weapon in Saudi Arabia to attack another Islamic country – even Iraq – could not be overcome.'

The B-52G force at Jeddah wound down from 9 March 1991, when Operation *Proud Return* began the redeployment of the 379th BW's personnel and aircraft to Wurtsmith.

MORON & FAIRFORD

Lurking behind coiled barbed wire at Fairford, B-52G 58-0245 *EQUIPOISE II* flew two missions with the 801st BW(P) before transferring to the 806th BW(P) at Fairford, with whom it flew nine more. The aircraft retained its small, neat nose art and its 2nd BW *Fleur de Lys* tail marking (*Terry Panopalis*)

EQUIPOISE II tucks up its landing gear as it gets airborne on one of its nine wartime sorties, toting a load of 750-lb M117 bombs. The aircraft's overall grey camouflage was a rarity during *Desert Storm*, when most aircraft still wore three-tone Strategic camouflage

Gen Norman Schwarzkopf, and his air commander Gen Chuck Horner, had always wanted more B-52s in-theatre, but Diego Garcia was too far from the action, imposing almost unmanageable sortie times on aircrews, while Saudi caution and reticence prevented basing more aircraft at Jeddah, or elsewhere in the kingdom. Schwarzkopf and Horner favoured using Cairo West as the base for a third B-52G provisional bombardment wing, until Egyptian objections forced a change of plan. Instead two provisional wings were established

B-52G 59-2580 *Sheriff's Posse II* was another 2nd BW 'Buff' which was deployed to Moron. The green of the aircraft's well-weathered Strategic camouflage had gained a reddish-brown tinge by the time it participated in *Desert Storm*. The B-52 wore a bomb-log consisting of a palm tree, a camel and 16 small black bombs (*Terry Panopalis*)

further away at existing USAFE bases in Europe, joining the action soon after the war began.

The first of these, the 801st BW(P), formed at Moron de la Frontera in Spain, close to the ancient city of Seville, under the command of the 2nd BW's CO, Col Ronald C Marcotte.

Personnel from the 2nd BW began establishing the new wing in late December 1990, and the first aircraft flew in during early January. Because of local political sensitivities, and especially because Spain did not want to be seen to be allowing the basing of bombers on its territory before hostilities actually began, the B-52s 'flight-planned' to Aviano, in Italy, and then diverted. They also used call-signs normally allocated to KC-10A Extender tankers.

It is understood that Moron's B-52s joined the bombing campaign on the fifth night of the war, once it was clear that sufficient tanker support was available.

Moron eventually had 20 Primary Aircraft Authorised (although some quoted PAA figures do not add up, listing 25 aircraft – seven from the 2nd BW, nine from 379th and nine from the 416th). A total of 27 aircraft deployed to Moron (not simultaneously), seven of which were drawn from the 2nd BW, two from the 42nd, one from the 97th, eight from the 379th and nine from the 416th.

Moron's B-52Gs flew 293 sorties (making the wing the third-placed B-52 unit) and 4397.8 flying hours (more than were flown in 841 sorties by the 1708th BW(P)), and dropped some 18,411 weapons out of an overall total of 72,289 delivered by B-52Gs during the war – a quantity exceeded only by the Jeddah-based wing.

Trailing a thick plume of black smoke, its gear tucking away, B-52G 58-0182 *What's Up DOC?* of the 379th BW is seen taking off on a *Desert Storm* sortie from Fairford in February 1991. The aircraft flew one mission from Moron and eight from the RAF base in Gloucestershire. The aircraft is laden down with M117 750-lb bombs (*Andy Bloom*)

Aircraft flying from Moron delivered 10,398 750-lb M117s, 6225 Mk 82s and 287 UK 1000-lb bombs. The 801st BW(P) dropped fewer CBUs than the Jeddah and Moron dets – 360 CBU-52s, 979 CBU-58s and 162 CBU-71/87/89s.

The Moron deployment ended on 17 April 1991.

FAIRFORD's 806th BW(P)

The smallest and shortest lived of the four B-52G-equipped provisional bomb wings was the 806th BW(P) at RAF Fairford.

Hastily created when it became clear that France would allow British-based 'Buffs' to overfly its territory, the unit was formed around a cadre provided by the 97th BW from Eaker AFB, and was commanded by the 97th's boss, Col George I Conlan.

Aircraft and aircrew for the Fairford detachment were drawn from the 524th BS/379th BW at Wurtsmith AFB, the 668th BS/416th BW at Griffiss AFB, the 62nd BS/2nd BW at Barksdale AFB and the 328th BTS/93rd BW at Castle AFB. The first B-52G for the new wing arrived at Fairford on 5 February – the day the new unit was designated the 806th BW(P).

The wing had eight Primary Aircraft Authorised, although once again the official figures did not add up, detailing one jet from the 2nd BW, one from the 93rd, six from the 379th and two from the 416th. Ten B-52s actually deployed to Fairford (not simultaneously), two from the

B-52G 59-2567 was one of the more anonymous looking 'Buffs' committed to *Desert Storm*, featuring no nose art, and with its 416th BW Statue of Liberty tail markings neatly, but effectively, overpainted. The aircraft flew nine missions from Moron, totalling 142 flying hours (*Terry Panopalis*)

Below
Laden with 750-lb M117 bombs, B-52G 57-6498 *Ace in the Hole* leads a 'Buff' cell out on a mission at Fairford. In the background, a RAF Gazelle flies a perimeter security patrol. This aircraft flew ten *Desert Storm* missions, totalling almost 151 flying hours (*Duncan Adams/Stewart Lewis*)

Above and right
When 58-0231 *High Roller* arrived at Fairford, it still wore the full colour Statue of Liberty tail markings of the 416th BW, although these were soon 'toned down' through the careful application of black paint – the outline of 'Lady Liberty' remained clear, however. This aircraft flew four missions, totalling 61.5 flying hours
(*Duncan Adams/Stewart Lewis*)

B-52G 57-6498 *Ace in the Hole* was another 416th BW aircraft whose Statue of Liberty tail markings were more comprehensively overpainted. The aircraft is seen here having its brake parachute repacked and tail guns serviced at a snowy Fairford
(*Duncan Adams/Stewart Lewis*)

2nd BW, six from 379th and two from the 416th. All the Fairford aircraft were intended to be '777' jets (ICSMS conventional aircraft), although in the event all were Cruise Missile Integrated!

Some 2000 tons of munitions arrived at Fairford from 6 February, 1158 tons of which would eventually be expended. The wing dropped 3008 of the 72,289 weapons expended by B-52Gs, comprising 2193 M117s, 560 Mk 82s, and 255 CBU-71/87/89s.

The wing became operational on 8 February. The first mission, using the call-sign 'Luxor', was launched the very next day, with three- and four-ship formations (with, initially, an extra 'air spare') being despatched daily until 27 February, except on 16 February and 26 February, when the missions were 'scrubbed'. On 22 February, the 806th BW(P)'s mission was launched from Jeddah, where the wing's four-ship cell of aircraft had diverted the day before.

Generally speaking, the missions proved straightforward, and the B-52s' serviceability was exemplary. The mission turnaround time pre-war had generally hovered around the 5.5-hour mark, but 90-minute turnarounds became routine at Fairford during the war. When the average sortie time was 16.3 hours, rapid turnarounds were essential.

There were, however, a handful of incidents. On 17 February, for example, 58-0204 *Special Delivery*, operating as 'Placid 73', suffered major hydraulic problems en route to the target. The captain was forced to jettison his bombload into the

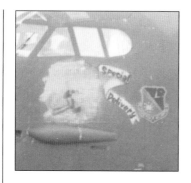

Unusually, 58-0204's nose art was partially overpainted, leaving the name *Special Delivery* intact. This 379th BW aeroplane completed six sorties, totalling 86.5 hours combat flying time (*Duncan Adams/Stewart Lewis and Andy Bloom*)

Left
Most 379th BW B-52Gs operating during *Desert Storm* retained their bold 'Triangle K' tail markings, seen here on 58-0247. The aircraft had its *High Plains Drifter* nose art (to port) overpainted in dark red. The bomber flew two *Desert Storm* missions, totalling 35 hours (*Duncan Adams/Stewart Lewis*)

Mediterranean, before diverting to Palermo. The aircraft returned to Fairford on 19 February. Despite unusually severe weather, which occasionally sprinkled Fairford with snow, there were relatively few weather diversions. Single aircraft diverted to Mildenhall (58-0231 *High Roller* on 18 February) and Jeddah (59-2579 on 27 February), and all four aircraft of 'Jenny' flight diverted to St Mawgan on 24 February. The wing's designated weather/refuelling diversions at Istres le Tube and Malpensa (Milan) were not used 'in anger'.

The B-52Gs of the 'Royal Gloucestershire Air Force' left Fairford between 1 and 9 March, having flown 62 sorties totalling 927.4 combat flying hours (some sources suggest that the hours total was rather higher, at 975.7 hours).

The Stratofortresses stationed furthest from their targets tied up a disproportionate number of the USAF's tankers, and the 806th's B-52Gs used aircraft from the 807th AREFS(P) at Mont de Marsan, and the 803rd AREFS(P) at Athens-Hellenikon.

Fairford would soon be used as a base for B-52s again, but these would be H-models, bombing targets in the Middle East and later in the Balkans. These missions, however, are the subject of the next B-52 volume in this series.

Above and below
B-52G 59-2589 *DARKEST HOUR* lost its nose art during the course of the war, the bold skull insignia being blanketed with glossy black paint. Fairford's 'Buffs' were the most 'censored', and the most likely to lose both nose art and tail markings, although 59-2589 retained its 'Triangle K' insignia throughout the war, flying ten sorties and logging 151.9 flying hours – more than any other 801st BW(P) jet (*Andy Bloom (nose art) and Terry Panopalis*)

B-52H IN *DESERT STORM*

L ike all previous 'Buff' variants, the B-52H could carry a limited range of conventional ordnance in its capacious bomb-bay, and on the old underwing AGM-128 Hound Dog pylons fitted with an I-Beam, rack adaptor and two Multiple Ejector Racks. The aircraft lacked the maritime and specialised weapons capabilities of some modified and upgraded B-52Gs, however, and at the time of *Desert Storm*, was unable to carry the Heavy Stores Adaptation Beam (HSAB), as used by conventional B-52Gs.

But unlike the older G-models, the B-52Hs had a new Common Strategic Rotary Launcher (CSRL) in the bomb-bay, allowing eight extra AGM-86 cruise missiles to be carried, in addition to the six mounted externally below each wing. And from June 1990, the H-model Stratofortresses also began to receive the new Convair AGM-129 Advanced Cruise Missile.

When *Desert Storm* began, the B-52H still had a primarily nuclear role, although crews did remain qualified in conventional missions, and were set to join the fray as the war ended (*USAF official*)

Two B-52Hs (60-0051 and 60-0052, or four aircraft, according to some sources) were modified to be able to accept a *Giant Fish* air-sampling module in the forward bomb-bay. The *Giant Fish* pod was originally called *Sea Fish*, and several Castle-based B-52Fs were configured to carry it during the 1960s.

The pod was moved to the B-52H when the B-52Fs were withdrawn from active use in the early 1970s, and the capability shifted to Carswell's H-models in about 1983.

The pod was designed to detect radioactive traces from nuclear tests or accidents, and could be rapidly installed at unit level, changing the selected aircraft from a standard atom-bomber into a dedicated air-sampling platform. The gunner's station was permanently modified with controls for the 900-kg sampling pod, which had five retractable sampling scoops. When a *Giant Fish* sortie was flown, the gunner was usually left behind, making room for two enlisted specialists who would travel to Castle from McClellan AFB for the flight.

An ex-B-52 groundcrewman who wished to remain anonymous told the author:

'I was a B-52H crew chief at Castle from 1980 to 1984, and I can remember helping to "split" the bomb-bay doors on at least three occasions in preparation for the loading of the fish pod. Most of the missions that were flown were simply training sorties, but I do recall a "live" mission in either 1982 or 1983, when an old Russian satellite that had radioactive material in it fell back into the earth's atmosphere. We had a "Buff" with the "fish pod" installed on alert so that air samples could be taken if the satellite came down in the Western hemisphere. The brass was serious about the mission. They even had the tail "stinger" loaded full of 20 mm ammunition.'

The *Giant Fish* B-52s were subsequently used for atmospheric monitoring missions in the wake of the 1986 Chernobyl nuclear reactor disaster, flying 12-14 hour sorties. The *Giant Fish*-equipped airframes and equipment went on to Fairchild when Carswell closed, and were finally assigned to Minot.

The *Giant Fish* aircraft were particularly unpopular with gunners, as one former H-model aircrewman later recalled.

'Being one of the last gunners, I definitely remember the *Giant Fish* aircraft. I hated flying in '0051 and '0052 because the *Giant Fish* control

What might have been – a B-52H carrying 500-lb bombs flies a conventional bombing mission. Had the war lasted a few days longer, B-52Hs from Stateside bases would have started to supplant the in-theatre B-52Gs (*Author's collection*)

unit was right in my face, and I kept bumping my right arm and shoulder into the damned thing all flight long. From a gunner's perspective, they were undoubtedly the two most uncomfortable aeroplanes to fly in. I flew those "Buffs" at Castle during training in 1978, and later at Carswell in 1986-90.'

Some reports suggested that the programme was terminated during the early 1990s, but other sources claim that *Giant Fish* may have been reinstated because of the shortfall in the USAF's air-sampling capability which resulted from the premature retirement of all but one WC-135 at the end of the Cold War.

Reports that two CONUS-based B-52Hs flew sorties in support of *Desert Storm* may have indicated that *Giant Fish* was being used to assess whether there had been any release of radioactive material from Iraqi facilities damaged by Coalition bombing, although this has never been officially confirmed by the US Department of Defense. Other conventionally configured B-52Hs came close to participating more actively in the operation.

Although they were SIOP assigned, SAC's B-52H units had the same conventional bombing capabilities as the CMI G-models, and as such, were just as able to participate in *Desert Storm*. Initially, though, the contribution made by the H-model wings took the form of personnel, who were sent through an abbreviated H to G conversion course (the so-called 'G-difference pipeline') with the 93rd BW – the B-52 replace-ment training unit at Castle AFB. The syllabus for this course consisted of two flying sorties and a brief groundschool session. Graduates would then be able to serve as B-52G replacement crews.

The war ended before most of the converted crews could be sent to Jeddah and Diego Garcia, although a handful did reach the provisional bomb wings. Two of these H-model crews from the 7th BW at Carswell AFB were deployed to Diego Garcia, and two more were deployed to Jeddah. One of these four crews did manage to fly a single combat sortie from Diego Garcia on the last night of the war, but, according to one veteran, 'the Jeddah guys were told by the 1708th BW(P) leadership there that they were only good enough to taxi the Gs out and back in for the "real" warriors'!

Further Carswell aircrew were undergoing conversion as the war ended. It has also been reported that at least one, and perhaps two,

The 7th BW at Carswell was preparing to launch a nine-ship mission from Carswell as the war ended. The aircraft would have hit targets in Iraq, before recovering to a forward location, presumably Jeddah (*David K Donald*)

Fairchild B-52H crews flew a single mission from one of the deployed locations (not Jeddah). There was also at least one crew from the 3909th SAES (1st CEVG) at Jeddah, who were dual-qualified on both the B-52G and the B-52H.

But by the time the war ended, the decision had already been taken to commit B-52H aircrew to action in their own aircraft. One Carswell H-model crewman remembered that:

'We were going through H to G conversion at Castle when the war ended, but my squadron commanding officer told us that we wouldn't have beaten the rest of the squadron into battle, as they were readying a nine-ship to launch from our base to ingress Iraq and then recover to a forward location.'

Another Carswell-based B-52H 'crew dog' recalled that:

'The H-model "Buffs" at Carswell were preparing to enter the *'Storm*. As I understand it, the plan was to fly the G-models during the first portion of the war, then, as they came due for phase inspection, the Gs would be rotated back to CONUS, rather than being phased in-theatre. The H-models would relieve them at that point. But the war ended before our Hs could join the fray.'

Had the Carswell B-52Hs deployed, they might have introduced a new weapon, as a former member of the 7th BW explained:

'I was working in the Flightline Avionics section at that time. We had just begun integration of the Popeye, and were setting up hardpoints for that missile on at least six of our B-52Hs. Our pilots discussed going on Scud patrols at medium/high altitude, and using the Popeye to eliminate Scud launch sites.

'There was also an electro-optical telescopic pod hooked up on at least one of the old hardpoints between the inboard and outboard engine clusters, usually between the Nos 2 and 3 engines. I received hardcopy orders to go to Jeddah to support the Hs in this capacity, but they were cancelled before we deployed.'

It has been suggested that the H-models would have been employed 'Scud hunting', using the AGM-142 'Have Nap' missile (two of which are carried by this aircraft), although this seems unlikely (*USAF official*)

CONCLUSIONS

Day after day during *Desert Storm*, USAF B-52Gs continued hammering Iraqi's Army and elite Republican Guard in the field. Around-the-clock bombing was a powerful psychological weapon, and ground forces were quickly worn down until they became demoralised and ineffective, or surrendered in droves. En masse desertions were directly attributed to the effects of B-52 bombing.

Because the B-52G achieved the remarkable statistic of dropping about 34 per cent of the ordnance expended during the war in spectacular fashion, and because only one aircraft (and three aircrew) was lost – and then not to enemy action – it was therefore easy to conclude that the aircraft had been an unqualified success during *Desert Storm*, and indeed that conclusion was reached by many analysts and observers post-war.

In terms of ordnance delivered, the relatively small force of B-52Gs deployed certainly performed impressively, especially in view of the relatively modest total number of sorties flown (1625, or just over 25 sorties per primary aircraft authorised). The B-52Gs accounted for about 30 per cent of the total Coalition bomb tonnage (and about 40 per cent of the USAF total), dropping 72,289 weapons weighing 27,000 tonnes.

B-52Gs delivered more bomb tonnage (32 million pounds of bombs) against strategic targets in the ELE, KBX, MIB, OCA and OIL target categories than any other platform.

In reality, the picture was rather more complicated, and while the B-52 was an undoubted success, it could have been used very much more effective. Indeed, the B-52 was officially judged to have been 'fully successful' against just 25 targets, and 'not fully successful' against 35 – the worst FS:NFS ratio (0.7:1) of any USAF platform in *Desert Storm*.

Post-war, SAC officially reported that the B-52 CEP had been inadequate. This inaccuracy resulted mainly from high winds, which severely affected unguided bomb ballistics during high-level operations (which had never been expected). A further error margin was introduced by a contractor who misidentified the ground coordinates of numerous targets. Thus, while B-52Gs delivered much more tonnage individually and as a force than any other aircraft, accuracy from high altitude was low.

Any assessment of exactly what the B-52 did or did not achieve must be preceded by the cautionary warning that the number of aircraft attacking the same targets, coupled with a lack of accurate and timely battle damage assessment, make it very difficult to isolate the B-52G's contribution, and as such any analysis must be partially subjective.

What the USAF called the KTO was ideally suited to the

A line-up of B-52Gs from the 1708th BW(P) at Jeddah, most of them wearing the monochromatic grey colour scheme and the SAC badge on the starboard forward fuselage. The 1708th accounted for the bulk of *Desert Storm* B-52 sorties (*Andy Bloom*)

employment of air power, with its vast, flat, open terrain making it easier to find targets. Although cloud cover and storms made for the poorest weather in the region for some 14 years, conditions were no worse than what would probably have been the best weather conditions expected in any other conflict. Moreover, until the ground war started, many Iraqi ground forces remained entrenched in fixed positions, permitting repeated strikes against them during the 40 days of air bombardment which preceded the ground assault.

Although only one B-52G was lost during *Desert Storm*, and none were downed as a result of enemy action, several aircraft were hit and badly damaged by both Iraqi and friendly fire. Five B-52Gs suffered 'significant' damage, two being hit or damaged by SAMs (one by an IR-guided missile) and two by AAA or shrapnel from exploding AAA. One aircraft lost two engines after a near-miss by an SA-3 missile, and another was hit by an unknown type of missile, but made it home safely.

Five B-52Gs damaged in 1706 sorties represented a damage rate of 0.0029 hits per sortie, which was high by *Desert Storm* standards. Indeed, only the A-6E (0.0031) and Tornado (0.0076) suffered worse.

Not included in the statistics were the single B-52G damaged by a hit from an AGM-88A HARM missile. This weapon was fired by a USAF F-4G that was undertaking defence suppression. Fortunately, the aircraft was able to land safely at Jeddah, although it played no further part in the war. Nor does the statistic include the B-52G lost on 3 February after a catastrophic electrical system failure while returning to Diego Garcia. While responding to the failure, improper fuel management on the part of the crew caused five engines to flame out. Three crewmembers ejected safely before the aircraft crashed into the Indian Ocean, but the remainder ejected too late and were killed.

It has been claimed that CENTAF bomber planners, more used to tactical fighter aircraft, employed the B-52 in a similar way, and failed to make the best use of its conventional capabilities. Instead of using the B-52 to attack fixed, large-area targets, where their large bomb capacity would have the most effect (such as supply depots and ammunition storage areas) pressure from ground force commanders led to their use against enemy troop concentrations opposite allied positions, primarily for psychological reasons. These sorties often required last-minute target changes. Gen Schwarzkopf agreed with his ground commanders that this was the best way to use the B-52, and duly overruled his Joint Force Air Component Commander.

Because few of the planners had any direct experience of the B-52G (which was, in any case, in its infancy in the conventional bombing role), it was not realised how many bombers would be needed to produce significant target damage. Post-war analysis indicated that the number of B-52Gs employed was often insufficient to achieve significant levels of damage, and the same targets frequently had to be struck over again.

The deployed B-52G force also faced logistics constraints which dramatically affected its effectiveness. Three of the four 'Buff' bases used during the war were more than 3600 miles away from the combat theatre, resulting in long, exhausting missions for the crews, and limiting the number of sorties which individual aircraft could fly to an average of about 0.6 sorties per day. This limitation was 'hidden' by the fact that the

The flying suit badge worn by some of the crews of the 806th BW(P). The tiny detachment at Fairford generated a host of flying suit badges, one based on a traditional 'RAF-type' crest, this one bearing the legend *Baghdad Firework Display 1991*. Yet another patch (seen on page 83) boasted a bold insignia based on the Union Jack and Stars and Stripes (*David K Donald*)

B-52s had nearly eight times the daily average munition delivery rate by comparison with aircraft like the F-117 (8.69 tons versus 1.10 tons) because of their greater carrying capability. Had all of the B-52s been based 'closer to the action', the tonnage delivered per day could have been even higher.

This might have caused further problems, however, since the supply system was barely able to

keep pace with the B-52G's high demand for munitions in any case. It has been claimed that this sometimes led to jets being despatched on sorties with munitions that were not well suited to mission needs. The USAF's official post-war report revealed that 'Operational planners with two *Desert Storm* B-52G units believed that they lacked an appropriate mix of munitions that would have given them a better chance of achieving mission objectives. Frequent, last-minute target changes also resulted in B-52Gs dropping less than the optimum munitions on some targets.'

Pre-positioned stocks of bombs in the CENTAF theatre were entirely inadequate to meet the needs of the B-52Gs deployed, and consisted primarily of older bombs and components that were intended for low-altitude operations, and which were considered unsuitable for the war's high-altitude tactics. Despite this, CENTAF did not authorise the shipment of B-52G munitions until late December 1990. This placed an unduly heavy reliance on airlift to support B-52G munitions needs during the war. Without airlift, it was claimed that 'Buffs' at one base would have run out of munitions entirely by the end of January.

Nor were the B-52G aircrew adequately prepared for the campaign they were expected to fight. Although the force had started to embrace conventional attack missions, most units were still nuclear orientated. The nuclear role had increasingly emphasised long-range, centrally planned strikes against fixed targets by single bombers operating autonomously, and often using stand-off weapons (primarily ALCMs). SAC had always emphasised low-altitude tactics as the best way to increase survivability.

The use of high-altitude tactics during *Desert Storm* revealed deficiencies in both equipment and training. The bombing system was

The B-52G squadrons were rightly proud of what they had achieved in *Desert Storm*. This is how the 416th BW's 668th BS summed it up during 1991 (*David K Donald*)

Later named *Beast of the East*, B-52G 59-2568 flew 206.5 hours from Moron in 13 combat sorties. The aircraft was stripped of nose art and its 416th BW tail markings, and is seen here just after the war, returning to the USA via Fairford, already minus its underwing pylons (*Duncan Adams/Stewart Lewis*)

not suited to high-level use, and this produced bombing inaccuracies, which were only exacerbated by the lack of suitable high-altitude-optimised weapons.

Although the jet's defensive system (intended to jam enemy radar) had recently been upgraded, it had to be supplemented with Vietnam-era jammers for high-level use. The latter had to be recovered from storage, and there were too few to equip all the B-52Gs. This meant that some jets could not be used in strikes against certain heavily defended targets.

Nor were the aircrews any better prepared, having gained little experience of operating with the kind of fighter/support packages provided to help defeat the Iraqi threat, or with AWACS and J-STARS. Crews were not used to reacting to the changing of targets, and lacked standardised procedures for attacking in formation. This meant that crews from different Stateside units were reluctant to fly together.

But probably the most significant B-52G training deficiency was the almost exclusive focus on low-altitude operations before the war. As a result, aircrew continued to use techniques that were more appropriate to the low-level environment, and were less proficient at procedures such as radar tuning that were required during higher-altitude operations.

Had the B-52Gs been used in a way which took greater advantage of their strengths, there is little doubt that greater damage could have been caused to the enemy at lower cost. But at the end of the day, the aircraft did do exactly what was asked of them, and thereby met the needs of the theatre commander. The official post-war assessment concluded that 'The B-52G fulfilled the objectives of the theatre commander without necessarily maximising its inherent capabilities.' But lessons were learned, and these ensured that when the B-52H went to war during the next decade, it would do so with even greater effectiveness.

Buffasaurus (58-0194) of the 379th BW flew 46 *Desert Storm* missions – one was launched from Wurtsmith, and the rest from Jeddah. The aircraft is seen here lining up for another mission with the 1708th BW(P)

Watched by the crew of a suitably camouflaged fire truck, an anonymous B-52G lifts off from Jeddah at the start of a mission against the Iraqi Republican Guard (*Andy Bloom*)

B-52G 57-6515 *Mohawk Warrior* of
the 416th BW flew four *Desert
Storm* missions from Moron,
totalling 64.9 combat flying hours.
Even without its heavy bombload,
the B-52G relied on a large-diameter
braking parachute to land within a
reasonable distance
(*Author's collection*)

Cluster bombs hang from the pylons
of 58-0255 as this ex-42nd BW
aircraft is prepared for one of its 55
Desert Storm sorties. The aircraft
flew in to Jeddah from Diego Garcia
on 17 January 1991, and eventually
logged 246.2 combat flying hours
(*Andy Bloom*)

Within months of the end of the
war, most of the veteran B-52Gs
were in, or heading for, the desert
boneyard at Davis-Monthan AFB,
Arizona, where they were cut up in
accordance with strategic arms
treaty provisions (*USAF official*)

APPENDICES

APPENDIX A

OPERATION *DESERT STORM* B-52 AIRFRAMES, UNITS, SORTIES AND FLYING HOURS

Serial	Parent unit	Deployed unit	Sorties	Flying hours	Notes
57-6472	379th BW	801st BW(P)	11	173.9	
57-6473	93rd BW	4300th BW(P)	18	249.9	
57-6474	379th BW	801st BW(P)	11	173.8	
57-6475	2nd BW	2nd BW	1	34.2	AGM-86C sortie 4
57-6476	93rd BW	4300th BW(P)	23	338.7	
57-6488	42nd BW	4300th BW(P)	22	334.0	
57-6492	379th BW	1708th BW(P)	1	16.1	deployed to Jeddah
57-6492	379th BW	1708th BW(P)	54	233.1	
57-6497	93rd BW	4300th BW(P)	24	339.3	
57-6498	416th BW	806th BW(P)	11	177.1	
57-6501	416th BW	801st BW(P)	6	95.2	deployed to Jeddah
57-6501	416th BW	1708th BW(P)	10	44.0	sub from Moron AB
57-6503	97th BW	801st BW(P)	1	15.9	only non-strategic radar
57-6508	2nd BW	801st BW(P)	5	79.2	
57-6509	2nd BW	801st BW(P)	3	40.5	deployed to Jeddah
57-6509	2nd BW	1708th BW(P)	29	134.5	sub from Moron AB
57-6515	416th BW	801st BW(P)	4	64.9	
57-6516	416th BW	801st BW(P)	11	173.1	
58-0159	379th BW	1708th BW(P)	1	17.5	deployed to Jeddah
58-0159	379th BW	1708th BW(P)	46	205.9	
58-0164	416th BW	801st BW(P)	6	77.8	deployed to Jeddah
58-0164	416th BW	1708th BW(P)	26	119.3	sub from Moron AB
58-0165	416th BW	801st BW(P)	25	358.5	1 abort, 1 recall
58-0168	379th BW	806th BW(P)	2	33.8	to Moron AB 3/2/91
58-0168	379th BW	801st BW(P)	9	142.1	
58-0170	416th BW	801st BW(P)	23	337.8	1 recall
58-0173	379th BW	1708th BW(P)	1	18.5	deployed to Jeddah
58-0173	379th BW	1708th BW(P)	42	190.6	
58-0175	379th BW	1708th BW(P)	1	17.4	deployed to Jeddah
58-0175	379th BW	1708th BW(P)	47	215.8	
58-0176	2nd BW	801st BW(P)	20	301.4	
58-0177	2nd BW	2nd BW	1	35.4	AGM-86C sortie 1
58-0181	2nd BW	801st BW(P)	25	355.1	1 recall
58-0182	379th BW	806th BW(P)	8	105.5	from Moron AB 22/2/91
58-0182	379th BW	801st BW(P)	1	16.1	transferred from RAF Fairford
58-0183	2nd BW	2nd BW	1	34.9	AGM-86C sortie 6
58-0185	2nd BW	2nd BW	1	34.6	AGM-86C sortie 7
58-0192	42nd BW	379th BW	1	17.6	deployed to Jeddah
58-0192	42nd BW	1708th BW(P)	49	216.0	
58-0194	379th BW	1708th BW(P)	1	15.8	deployed to Jeddah
58-0194	379th BW	1708th BW(P)	46	208.2	
58-0195	42nd BW	801st BW(P)	2	32.5	1 abort
58-0195	42nd BW	4300th BW(P)	1	10.7	deployed to Jeddah 17/1/91
58-0195	42nd BW	1708th BW(P)	46	194.1	from Diego Garcia 17/1/91
58-0197	42nd BW	4300th BW(P)	17	254.8	
58-0202	42nd BW	4300th BW(P)	18	278.7	
58-0203	93rd BW	379th BW	1	15.9	deployed to Jeddah
58-0203	93rd BW	1708th BW(P)	57	245.2	
58-0204	379th BW	806th BW(P)	6	86.5	2 aborts, 1 divert to Jeddah
58-0206	42nd BW	4300th BW(P)	14	193.7	
58-0212	93rd BW	4300th BW(P)	17	262.9	
58-0213	93rd BW	4300th BW(P)	26	365.3	

58-0216	42nd BW	4300th BW(P)	24	347.0	
58-0217	379th BW	801st BW(P)	12	188.4	
58-0218	42nd BW	379th BW	1	18.9	deployed to Jeddah
58-0218	42nd BW	1708th BW(P)	28	122.0	
58-0218	42nd BW	801st BW(P)	1	15.3	transferred from Jeddah
58-0221	93rd BW	4300th BW(P)	17	246.3	
58-0226	42nd BW	4300th BW(P)	1	10.6	transferred to Jeddah 17/1/91
58-0226	42nd BW	1708th BW(P)	38	168.0	from Diego Garcia 17/1/91
58-0227	379th BW	801st BW(P)	12	193.0	
58-0230	42nd BW	4300th BW(P)	24	346.5	
58-0231	416th BW	806th BW(P)	4	61.5	
58-0233	93rd BW	4300th BW(P)	18	241.9	
58-0237	379th BW	806th BW(P)	9	137.7	
58-0238	2nd BW	2nd BW	1	33.9	AGM-86C sortie 5
58-0241	42nd BW	4300th BW(P)	7	99.2	
58-0242	93rd BW	4300th BW(P)	23	314.5	
58-0245	2nd BW	801st BW(P)	2	29.0	transferred to RAF Fairford 5/2/91
58-0245	2nd BW	806th BW(P)	9	133.0	from Moron AB 5/2/91, and 1 abort and 1 divert to Jeddah
58-0247	379th BW	806th BW(P)	3	51.9	
58-0248	93rd BW	4300th BW(P)	1	4.5	battle damage 17/1/91
58-0249	379th BW	801st BW(P)	10	160.6	
58-0250	42nd BW	4300th BW(P)	17	214.8	
58-0253	42nd BW	4300th BW(P)	1	11.1	transferred to Jeddah 17/1/91
58-0253	42nd BW	1708th BW(P)	52	214.6	from Diego Garcia 17/1/91
58-0255	42nd BW	4300th BW(P)	1	11.5	transferred to Jeddah 17/1/91
58-0255	42nd BW	1708th BW(P)	55	246.2	from Diego Garcia 17/1/91
58-0257	42nd BW	4300th BW(P)	1	11.4	transferred to Jeddah 17/1/91
58-0257	42nd BW	1708th BW(P)	55	246.1	from Diego Garcia 17/1/91
58-0258	93rd BW	4300th BW(P)	17	261.6	
59-2564	2nd BW	2nd BW	1	35.0	AGM-86C sortie 2
59-2565	93rd BW	4300th BW(P)	17	211.4	
59-2567	416th BW	801st BW(P)	9	142.0	
59-2568	416th BW	801st BW(P)	13	206.5	
59-2569	93rd BW	4300th BW(P)	23	340.3	
59-2570	93rd BW	379th BW	1	18.4	deployed to Jeddah
59-2570	93rd BW	1708th BW(P)	54	246.3	
59-2572	93rd BW	4300th BW(P)	14	190.5	
59-2573	42nd BW	4300th BW(P)	17	234.3	
59-2579	379th BW	801st BW(P)	12	185.4	
59-2579	2nd BW	806th BW(P)	2	31.3	from Moron AB 24/2/91
59-2580	2nd BW	801st BW(P)	17	236.0	1 abort
59-2582	2nd BW	2nd BW	1	34.3	AGM-86C sortie 3
59-2583	416th BW	801st BW(P)	7	91.1	transferred to Jeddah
59-2583	416th BW	1708th BW(P)	37	157.6	sub from Moron AB
59-2585	42nd BW	4300th BW(P)	1	12.2	transferred to Jeddah 17/1/91 due to possible HARM fratricide
59-2585	42nd BW	1708th BW(P)	22	94.8	from Diego Garcia 17/1/91
59-2588	93rd BW	4300th BW(P)	5	71.1	
59-2589	379th BW	806th BW(P)	10	151.9	
59-2590	2nd BW	801st BW(P)	25	355.4	1 abort
59-2591	379th BW	801st BW(P)	10	157.2	1 abort
59-2593	42nd BW	4300th BW(P)	4	62.5	crashed 3/2/91
59-2595	93rd BW	4300th BW(P)	23	307.1	
59-2598	93rd BW	379th BW	1	17.7	deployed to Jeddah
59-2598	93rd BW	1708th BW(P)	48	208.4	
59-2599	93rd BW	4300th BW(P)	23	347.1	
Totals			**1672**	**15990**	

APPENDIX B

OPERATION *DESERT STORM* B-52 UNITS

Apart from the *Senior Surprise* aircraft, the B-52Gs used during *Desert Storm* were deployed from their CONUS bases to four Forward Operating Locations, where they formed the basis of four provisional bomb wings. Each FOL and provisional wing was formed around a cadre from one CONUS-based unit, although in each case aircraft and aircrew were drawn from several wings. Together, the four provisional wings had a notional complement of 64 aircraft (20 each at Jeddah and Diego Garcia, 18 at Moron and just six at Fairford). With aircraft shifting between FOLs and going back and forth to and from maintenance, larger numbers (about 75) were actually deployed, although not simultaneously.

Provisional Wings	Forward Operating Locations	Sorties	Combat Hours
801st BW(P)	Moron AB, Spain	293	4397.8
806th BW(P)	RAF Fairford, England	62	927.4
1708th BW(P)	Jeddah AB, Saudi Arabia	841	3709.4
4300th BW(P)	Diego Garcia, Indian Ocean	459	6525.4
Totals:		**1655**	**15,560**

801st BW(P), MORON AB, SPAIN

Formed around a nucleus provided by the 2nd BW at Barksdale, and commanded by that wing's CO, Col Ronald C Marcotte, the 801st BW(P) also drew aircraft and crews from the 524th BS/379th BW at Wurtsmith AFB, the 668th BS/416th BW at Griffiss AFB, and from the 69th BS/42nd BW at Loring. One aircraft (57-6503 – the only B-52G sent into combat lacking a strategic radar) from the 340th BS/97th BW at Eaker AFB.

57-6508	*Outhouse Mouse*	2nd BW
57-6509	*Nine Oh Nine II*	2nd BW
58-0176		2nd BW
58-0181	*The Witch*	2nd BW
58-0245	*Equipoise II*	2nd BW
59-2580	*Sheriff's Posse II*	2nd BW
59-2590	*Better Duck*	2nd BW
58-0195		42nd BW
58-0218		42nd BW
57-6503	*Superstitious Aloysius*	97th BW
57-6472	*Mad Dog*	379th BW
57-6474	*Lone Wolf*	379th BW
58-0168	*Treasure Hunter*	379th BW
58-0182	*What's Up Doc*	379th BW
58-0217	*Liberator*	379th BW
58-0249	*Urban Renewal*	379th BW
59-2579		379th BW
59-2591	*Sudden Impact/Sweet Revenge*	379th BW
57-6501	*Ragin Red*	416th BW
57-6515	*Mohawk Warrior*	416th BW
57-6516	*Ultimate Warrior*	416th BW
58-0164	*SAC Time*	416th BW
58-0165		416th BW
58-0170	*Special Delivery II*	416th BW
59-2567		416th BW
59-2568	*Beast of the East*	416th BW
59-2583	*Rushin Nightmare*	416th BW

806th BW(P), RAF FAIRFORD, ENGLAND

The 806th BW(P) was formed around a cadre of air- and groundcrews provided by the B-52G-equipped 97th BW at Eaker AFB, and was commanded by Col George I Conlan. Stratofortresses and aircrew were drawn from the 524th BS/379th BW at Wurtsmith AFB, the 668th BS/416th BW at Griffiss AFB, the 62nd and 596th BS/2nd BW at Barksdale AFB and the 328th BTS/93rd BW at Castle AFB.

58-0245	*Equipoise II*	2nd BW
59-2579		2nd BW
58-0168	*Treasure Hunter*	379th BW
58-0182	*What's Up Doc*	379th BW
58-0204	*Special Delivery*	379th BW
58-0237	*Daffy's Destruction*	379th BW
58-0247	*High Plain's Drifter*	379th BW
59-2589	*Darkest Hour*	379th BW
57-6498	*Ace in the Hole*	416th BW
58-0231	*High Roller*	416th BW

1708th BW(P), KING ABDUL AZIZ IAP, JEDDAH (JEDDAH NEW), SAUDI ARABIA

The lead unit within the 1708th BW(P) was the 524th BS/379th BW from Wurtsmith AFB. Aircraft and crews were also drawn from the 62nd and 596th BS/2nd BW at Barksdale AFB, the 69th BS/42nd BW at Loring AFB, the 328th BS/93rd BW at Castle AFB and the 668th BS/416th BW at Griffiss AFB. B-52 operations were not possible at Jeddah before the war, so the wing gained its aircraft when the conflict began. Six aircraft transferred from Diego Garcia to Jeddah on 17 January, and ten more flew in from Wurtsmith, attacking targets en route. Although launched from Wurtsmith and flown by 379th BW crews, three of the ten aircraft came from Castle AFB, and two from Loring AFB.

57-6509	*Nine Oh Nine II*	2nd BW
58-0192		42nd BW
58-0195		42nd BW
58-0218		42nd BW
58-0226	*Wreckin' Crew*	42nd BW
58-0253		42nd BW
58-0255		42nd BW
58-0257		42nd BW
59-2585		42nd BW
58-0203		93rd BW
59-2570	*Ole Baldy*	93rd BW
59-2598		93rd BW
57-6492	*Old Crow Express*	379th BW
58-0159	*Alley Oops Bold Assault*	379th BW
58-0173	*Let's Make a Deal*	379th BW
58-0175	*Viper*	379th BW
58-0194	*Buffasaurus*	379th BW
57-6501	*Ragin Red*	416th BW
58-0164	*SAC Time*	416th BW
59-2583	*Rushin Nightmare*	416th BW

4300th BW(P), DIEGO GARCIA, BRITISH INDIAN OCEAN TERRITORY INDIAN OCEAN

The lead unit for the 4300th BW(P) was the 69th BS/42nd BW from Loring AFB, although aircraft were also drawn from the 328th BS/93rd BW at Castle AFB. Six aircraft transferred from Diego Garcia to Jeddah on 17 January 1991, and they were themselves replaced by six B-52Gs transferred in from the 1500th SW(P) on Guam.

57-6488		42nd BW
58-0195		42nd BW
58-0197		42nd BW
58-0202		42nd BW
58-0206		42nd BW
58-0216		42nd BW
58-0226	*Wreckin' Crew*	42nd BW
58-0230	*Black Widow*	42nd BW
58-0241		42nd BW
58-0250		42nd BW
58-0253		42nd BW
58-0255		42nd BW
58-0257		42nd BW
59-2573		42nd BW
59-2585		42nd BW
59-2593		42nd BW
57-6473	*Hard T'get*	93rd BW
57-6476		93rd BW
57-6497		93rd BW
58-0212		93rd BW
58-0213		93rd BW
58-0221		93rd BW
58-0233		93rd BW
58-0242		93rd BW
58-0248	*In Harm's Way*	93rd BW
58-0258		93rd BW
59-2565		93rd BW
59-2569		93rd BW
59-2572		93rd BW
59-2588		93rd BW
59-2595		93rd BW
59-2599		93rd BW

APPENDIX C

B-52G/H UNITS 1990–94

In 1990, Strategic Air Command had two numbered Air Forces, namely the Eighth, headquartered at Barksdale AFB, and controlling units based in the eastern USA, and the Fifteenth, headquartered at March AFB, and controlling units in the western USA. Thus, the Eighth Air Force controlled B-52 wings at K I Sawyer AFB, Michigan (410th BW), Wurtsmith AFB, Michigan (379th BW), Griffiss AFB, New York (416th BW), Loring AFB, Maine (42nd BW), Eaker AFB, Arkansas (97th BW), Barksdale AFB, Louisiana (2nd BW) and Carswell AFB, Texas (7th BW). The Fifteenth Air Force controlled the B-52 wings at Fairchild AFB, Washington (92nd BW), Minot AFB, North Dakota (5th BW) and Castle AFB, California (93rd BW).

One squadron of B-52s remained outside SAC. In November 1986, SAC had redesignated the 43rd SW at Andersen AFB, Guam, as the 43rd BW. The wing then began to transition from the nuclear alert role into a lead contingency wing, completing the process in October 1988. The 43rd BW began redeploying to Stateside bases in late 1989, and Andersen AFB transitioned from SAC to Pacific Air Forces control.

Of these units, only the 42nd BW was exclusively dedicated to conventional bombing operations. The similarly assigned 320th BW had inactivated in September 1989, and the 43rd followed before *Desert Storm* began in September 1990. But the remaining units increasingly assumed a conventional commitment alongside their nuclear role, and, indeed, in September 1991, a Presidential order ended 34 years of 24-hour ground alert for SAC's bomber/tanker force.

Air Combat Command (ACC) took over SAC's strategic bombers in June 1992, when 84 B-52Gs were still in service, alongside 95 B-52Hs, although the G-models were already counting down to retirement. Nine wings were consolidated into just two during the same period, while the Fifteenth Air Force was relieved of its assignment to SAC and assigned to Air Mobility Command on 1 January 1992, leaving just the 'Mighty Eighth'. The B-52G-equipped 2nd BW gained B-52Hs, as did the 416th, while the 42nd, 93rd and 379th BWs disbanded, and the 366th (34th BS) discarded its B-52s altogether. The B-52H-equipped 7th, 92nd, 410th and 416th BWs also disbanded, leaving only the 2nd and 5th BWs, whose subsequent combat record will be described in a future volume.

2nd BW

Barksdale's 2nd BW had been unusual in having two squadrons, with the 20th BS assigned conventional duties, while the 596th stood alert with ALCM-armed aircraft. The B-52G-equipped 62nd BS was replaced by the B-52H-equipped 20th BS (from Carswell) on 18 December 1992, and inactivated on 18 January 1993. The B-52G-equipped 596th BS was replaced by the B-52H-equipped 96th BS on 1 October 1992, and was inactivated soon afterwards. During the ACC era, the 2nd BW has used the tailcode 'LA', with a variety of squadron fin bands. From 1 October 1993, Barksdale also hosted the AFRes 917th BW, which used the tailcode 'BD' and a blue/yellow checkered tail stripe.

5th BW

The 5th BW's 23rd BS took its aircraft off alert status in September 1991, taking over a conventional role. As part of the realignment of the B-52 force, the 5th BW gained the 72nd BS from 1 December 1994. In the ACC era, the 5th BW has used the tailcode 'MT', and initially used a red and white 'candy stripe' tail band, before individual squadron fin markings were introduced.

7th BW

The 7th BW's B-52s wore a tail stripe on which was superimposed the skull of a Texan Longhorn. Its two squadrons were primarily assigned to the strategic strike role, using the AGM-86 ALCM. In ACC service, only one of Carswell's

B-52s used the assigned tailcode 'CW' before the wing lost its last B-52 on 18 December 1992. The 9th BS inactivated on 15 August and the 20th BS moved to Barksdale on 18 December. The wing then moved to Dyess without personnel or equipment and took over the identity of the former 96th BW, with B-1Bs.

42nd BW

By the time the B-52G went to war over Iraq, the 42nd BW was the only remaining unit dedicated to conventional operations (although others were transitioning to the conventional role). Its aircraft wore a moose's head badge, superimposed on a silhouette of the state of Maine, and usually with the word Loring following the line of the rudder. Some aircraft had a simplified moose head badge with a bomb in its mouth, and no Maine silhouette.

42nd BW B-52Gs and aircrew deployed to Diego Garcia with the 4300th BW(P), flew 960 missions (485 combat) in 44 days, and dropped 12,588,766 lbs of bombs, while further aircraft and aircrew deployed to the 1708th BW(P) at Jeddah..

The wing's aircraft exchanged their moose head badge for an 'LZ' tailcode during the ACC period, together with a red-trimmed black fin cap containing the words '42nd Bomb Wing'. The wing inactivated at Loring on 30 September 1994 after the 69th BS had inactivated on 31 December 1993. The last B-52G left for AMARC on 8 March 1994.

92nd BW

The 92nd BW's 325th BS flew the B-52H until inactivated on 1 July 1994, when the parent wing was redesignated as a refuelling unit. On 1 September 1991 the 92nd BW(Heavy) was redesignated as the 92nd Wing, but on 1 June 1992 it became part of the newly formed ACC, and was redesignated again as the 92nd BW. The unit ended B-52 alert duties in September 1992, and from February 1993 took over the *Giant Fish* mission for the Department of Energy. During the ACC period, the wing used the tailcode 'FC', initially with a blue tail stripe, and from early 1993 with a red/black checkered tail stripe. In SAC's last days, the wing's Stratofortresses had been decorated with a huge 'seahawk' head inspired by the emblem of the American Football team the *Seattle Seahawks*.

93rd BW

The 93rd BW was SAC's first B-52 Stratofortress heavy bomber wing. Although it was considered an operational unit, its primary mission was transition training for new B-52 crews. As the B-52 training unit, it latterly parented the 328th BS (which inactivated on 15 June 1994) and the 329th Combat Crew Training Squadron (inactivated on 17 July 1994). Its aircraft initially wore a stylised 'castle' fin badge, although during the ACC period aircraft wore 'CA' tailcodes and a blue tail stripe. The 93rd BW's 58-0240 was the last B-52G to be retired, flying to AMARC on 3 May 1994.

97th BW

One of the 97th BW's B-52s earned the distinction of flying the last mission over a target in Cambodia on 15 August 1973, marking the end of the USAF's bombing campaign in Southeast Asia.

Committed to the strategic role using the AGM-86B air-launched cruise missile (ALCM), the wing expanded its mission to include conventional bombing, sea search and surveillance, as well as aerial mining from 1987.

Although only one of its aircraft deployed to participate in *Desert Storm*, the wing, and its aircrew, were more heavily involved. Six of the wing's bombers and crews assumed ground alert duty at Wurtsmith AFB, relieving the 379th BW, and on 1 February 1991, after practising high-altitude bombing missions at the Nellis AFB test range, major elements of the 97th deployed to RAF Fairford, UK, where they formed the backbone of the 806th BW(P).

The wing was redesignated as the 97th Wing on 1 September 1991, and inactivated on 1 April 1992, before the formation of ACC. The wing's aircraft carried a very discreet 'flaming spear' badge on the tail fin.

366th Wing
The B-52G-equipped 34th BS was assigned to the 366th Wing from 1 July 1992 until 4 April 1994, although it was based at Castle AFB as a 'Geographically Separated Unit', rather than at the 366th Wing's Mountain Home, Idaho, base. It was the only B-52G unit equipped with AGM-142. The squadron's aircraft wore the tailcode 'MO' and a black tail stripe with a red Thunderbird superimposed.

379th BW
Despite being assigned to the nuclear strike role using the AGM-86 ALCM, the 379th was destined to play a vital role in *Desert Storm*. At the end of January 1991, six of the 97th BW's bombers and crews assumed ground alert duty at Wurtsmith AFB, allowing the 379th BW to participate in *Desert Storm*. Despite its impressive record, the Base Realignment And Closure (BRAC) commission recommended the closure of Wurtsmith in July 1991. The 524th BS inactivated on 15 December 1992, and the parent 379th ceased operations on 31 December 1992, inactivating on 15 June 1993. The 379th was not part of ACC long enough to gain tailcodes and new markings, and its aircraft continued to carry the distinctive 'Triangle K' emblem first applied to its B-17s at Kimbolton in World War 2!

410th BW
The 410th Bomb Wing at KI Sawyer AFB did not participate in *Desert Storm*. The wing was the first to employ the AGM-129 Advanced Cruise Missile.

Its B-52Hs wore a discreet 'rainbow' badge on their tail fins. The 410th BW's 644th BS lost its last two B-52Hs on 15 November 1994, and inactivated on 21 November. The 410th BW inactivated on 30 November. In the ACC era, the unit used the 'KI' tailcode, with a rainbow tail band.

416th BW
During *Desert Storm*, the 416th BW's B-52s, and crews, flew with the 801st, 806th and 1708th BW(P)s, and flew 148 combat sorties (11,000 flying hours) dropping 6274 bombs (4,394,350 lbs). As a SAC unit, the 416th BW decorated its B-52Gs with a massive representation of the Statue of Liberty, flanked by the word 'Griffiss' and a pair of cheatlines (the name and cheatlines were sometimes repeated on the underwing fuel tanks). Groundcrew information was displayed on a silhouette of the state of New York – black on camouflaged aircraft and in outline form on grey-painted jets. The wing's 668th BS was the first B-52G unit to be equipped with the AGM-86 ALCM, but increasingly practised conventional mass tactics from 'austere' bases following *Desert Storm*.

The 416th BW's 668th BS traded its B-52Gs for H-models in 1991, and used these until inactivated on 1 January 1995. The BRAC Commission voted to realign Griffiss AFB, stripping the base of its active flying mission in June 1993. The 416th OG inactivated on the same day as the 668th BS, and the 416th Wing followed on 30 September. The H-models wore GR tailcodes and a red and white tail stripe in place of the statue of liberty tail marking used previously.

APPENDIX D

B-52G STRATOFORTRESS NAMES AND NOSE ART

57-6468 *Eldership*
57-6469 *City of Sacramento*
57-6470 *Screaming for Vengeance*
57-6471 *Tantalizing Take Off*
57-6472 *Mad Dog*
57-6473 *Hard t'get*
57-6474 *Lone Wolf*
57-6475 *MIAMI Clipper II*
57-6477 *A Certain Fury*
57-6478 *Stars and Stripes*
57-6480 *The Big Stick*
57-6483 *Ragin' Cajun*
57-6485 *Miss Wing Ding II*
57-6488 *Shady Lady*
57-6488 *Wild Thing*
57-6489 *Express Delivery*
57-6490 *Phantom Four Ninety*
57-6491 *Little Patches*
57-6492 *Old Crow Express*
57-6498 *Ace in the Hole*
57-6499 *Against the Wind*
57-6501 *Ragin Red*
57-6502 *Night Stalker*
57-6503 *Superstitious Aloysius*
57-6504 *Snake Eyes*
57-6505 *Destination Devastation*
57-6506 *Command Decision*
57-6508 *Out House Mouse II*
57-6509 *Queen Andrea Hart of Holiday in Dixie*
57-6509 *Nine O Nine II*
57-6511 *Diabolical Angel*
57-6513 *Memphis Belle II*
57-6514 *Cottonball Express*
57-6514 *Royal Flush*
57-6515 *Mohawk Warrior*
57-6516 *Ultimate Warrior*
57-6517 *Buffalo Gal II*
57-6518 *Leo II*
57-6520 *Ten Hi*
58-0159 *Alley Oops Bold Assault*
58-0160 *Midnight Marauder*
58-0162 *Thunder Struck*
58-0163 *Dragon Lady*
58-0164 *SAC Time*
58-0165 *Rolling Thunder*
58-0166 *Mission Completed*
58-0168 *Treasure Hunter*
58-0170 *Special Delivery II*
58-0171 *Lil Peach II*
58-0172 *The Negotiator*
58-0173 *Lets Make a Deal*
58-0175 *Viper*
58-0177 *PETIE 3RD*
58-0178 *Old Soldier*
58-0180 *The Flyin' Pig*
58-0181 *The Witch*
58-0182 *What's Up Doc ?*
58-0183 *Valkyrie*

58-0184 *Miss Ouachita II*
58-0185 *El Lobo II*
58-0186 (unnamed, but with female nose art)
58-0189 *Special Kay*
58-0191 *Bearin' Arms*
58-0192 *East Coast Outlaw*
58-0193 *Iron Maiden*
58-0194 *Buffasaurus*
58-0195 *Eternal Guardian*
58-0198 *California Star*
58-0200 *Wolverine Warrior*
58-0204 *Special Delivery*
58-0205 *The Wild Hare 2*
58-0206 *Cultured Vulture*
58-0206 *Texas Ranger*
58-0207 *City of Merced*
58-0210 *Conceived for Liberty*
58-0211 *Miss Ouachita*
58-0214 *City of Goldsboro*
58-0214 *Ack-Ack Annie*
58-0216 *Thunder Struck*
58-0217 *Liberator*
58-0220 *Night Hawk VI*
58-0222 *Triple Deuce*
58-0223 *Spirit of America*
58-0226 *Wreckin Crew*
58-0227 *Urban Renewal*
58-0227 *The Black Buzzard*
58-0229 *Sioux Warrior*
58-0230 *Son of Killroy*
58-0230 *Black Widow*
58-0231 *High Roller*
58-0233 *Chow Hound*
58-0234 *Strangelove*
58-0235 *Spirit of Mt Rushmore'*
58-0236 *Lucky 13*
58-0237 *Daffy's Destruction*
58-0237 *The Blytheville Storm*
58-0238 *Miss Fit II*
58-0239 *Loring Moose Goose'*
58-0244 *Hellsadroppin*
58-0245 *Equipoise II*
58-0247 *High Plains Drifter*
58-0247 *Dream Warrior*
58-0248 *In Harm's Way*
58-0249 *Urban Renewal*
58-0250 *Surprise Attack II*
58-0250 *Screamin' Eagle*
58-0251 *Honeysuckle Rose*
58-0252 *Sagittarius II*
58-0254 *Damage Inc*
58-0255 *Guardian of Peace*
58-0257 *The Moose is Loose*
58-0257 *First Strike*
58-0258 *Claim Buster*
59-2566 *The Wild Potato*
59-2568 *Beast of the East*
59-2570 *City of Bossier City*

59-2570 *Ole Baldy*
59-2573 *Avenger*
59-2575 *Large Marge*
59-2580 *Sheriff's Posse II*
59-2581 *Grand Illusion*
59-2582 *Grim Reaper II*
59-2583 *Rushin' Nightmare*
59-2584 *Memphis Belle III*
59-2585 *Swashbuckler*
59-2585 *Yossarian's Question*
59-2587 *Stratofortress Rex*
59-2588 *The Eagle's Wrath*
59-2589 *Darkest Hour*
59-2589 *War Bitch*
59-2590 *Better Duck*
59-2591 *Sudden Impact*
59-2591 *Sweet Revenge*
59-2592 *The Lavender Panther*
59-2594 *Memphis Belle III*
59-2596 *Eager Beaver*
59-2598 *Dangerous Toys*
59-2599 *Wild Thing*
59-2601 *Itzagoer*
59-2602 *Yankee Doodle II*

APPENDIX E

2nd BW *SECRET SQUIRREL* CREWS

B-52G 58-0177 *PETIE 3rd*
'Doom 31' Sortie 1
Crew S-91
Airborne Mission Commander: **Lt Col John H Beard***
Aircraft commander: **Capt Michael G Wilson**
Co-pilot: **1Lt Kent R Beck**
Radar navigator: **Capt George W Murray III**
Navigator: **1Lt Mark W VanDoren**
Electronic warfare officer: **Capt Richard P Holt**
Gunner: **Sgt Dale R Jackson**
Augmentee navigator: **Capt Lee S Richie Jr**
(*Beard also acted as the augmentee pilot)

B-52G 59-2564 (no name or nose art)
'Doom 32' Sortie 2
Crew E-54
Aircraft commander: **Capt John P Romano**
Co-pilot: **Capt Eric K Hayden**
Radar navigator: **Capt Steven R Hess**
Navigator: **Capt Toby L Corey**
Electronic warfare officer: **1Lt Robert C Lightner**
Gunner: **Airman First Class Steven L Gramling**
Augmentee pilot: **Maj Steven E Jackson**
Augmentee navigator: **Capt Alan C Teauseau**

B-52G 59-2582 *Grim Reaper II*
'Doom 33' Sortie 3
Crew R-53
Aircraft commander: **Capt Charles E Jones Jr**
Co-pilot: **Capt Warren G Ward**
Radar navigator: **Capt Patrick Hobday**
Navigator: **1Lt Aaron E Hattabaugh**
Electronic warfare officer: **Capt Kevin M Williams**
Gunner: **Sgt William J McCutchen**
Augmentee pilot: **Maj William H Weller**
Augmentee navigator: **Maj Bruce F Blood**

B-52G 57-6475 *MIAMI Clipper II*
'Doom 34' Sortie 4
Crew E-83
Aircraft commander: **Capt Bernard S Morgan**
Co-pilot: **1Lt Michael C Branche**
Radar navigator: **Capt John S Ladner**
Navigator: **1Lt Andre J Mouton**
Electronic warfare officer: **Capt James L Morriss III**
Gunner: **Airman First Class Guy W Modgling**

Augmentee pilot: **Capt Steven E Bass**
Augmentee navigator: **Maj Wesley H Bain**

B-52G 58-0238 *Miss Fit II*
'Doom 35' Sortie 5
Crew E-81
Aircraft commander: **Capt Marcus S Myers**
Co-pilot: **1Lt Michael L Hansen**
Radar navigator: **Capt David J Byrd**
Navigator: **1Lt Don E Broyles**
Electronic warfare officer: **Capt Todd H Mathes**
Gunner: **Sgt Martin R VanBuren**
Augmentee pilot: **Capt Chadwick H Barr Jr**
Augmentee navigator: **Capt Donald Van Slambrook**

B-52G 58-0183 *Valkyrie*
'Doom 36' Sortie 6
Crew S-92
Aircraft commander: **Capt Alan W Moe**
Co-pilot: **Capt David T Greer Jr**
Radar navigator: **Capt Blaise M Martinick**
Navigator: **1Lt John S Pyles**
Electronic warfare officer: **Capt Anthony Bothwell**
Gunner: **Sgt Danny L Parker**
Augmentee pilot: **Capt Joseph M Hasbrouck**
2nd augmentee pilot: **Maj Steven D Weilbrenner**
Augmentee navigator: **Capt Matthew G Casella**

B-52G 58-0185 *El Lobo II*
'Doom 37' Sortie 7
Crew S-93
Aircraft commander: **Capt Stephen D Sicking**
Co-pilot: **1Lt Russell F Mathers**
Radar navigator: **Capt Floyd W Gowans**
Navigator: **1Lt Gregory D Moss**
Electronic warfare officer: **Capt Paul M Benson**
Gunner: **S/Sgt William J LeClair**
Augmentee pilot: **Capt Steven W Kirkpatrick**
Augmentee navigator: **Maj Fredrick D Van Wicklin**

Both drawings on this spread are of a B-52G
Stratofortress, and are to 1/252nd scale (as are
the drawings on page 90)

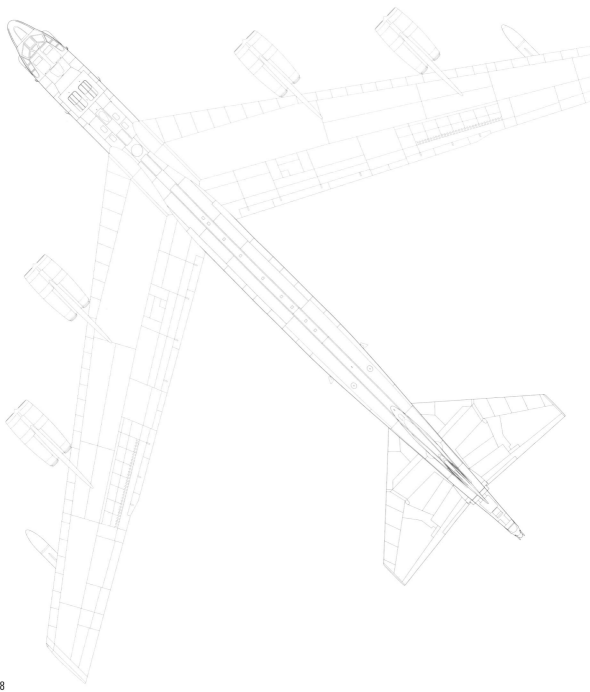

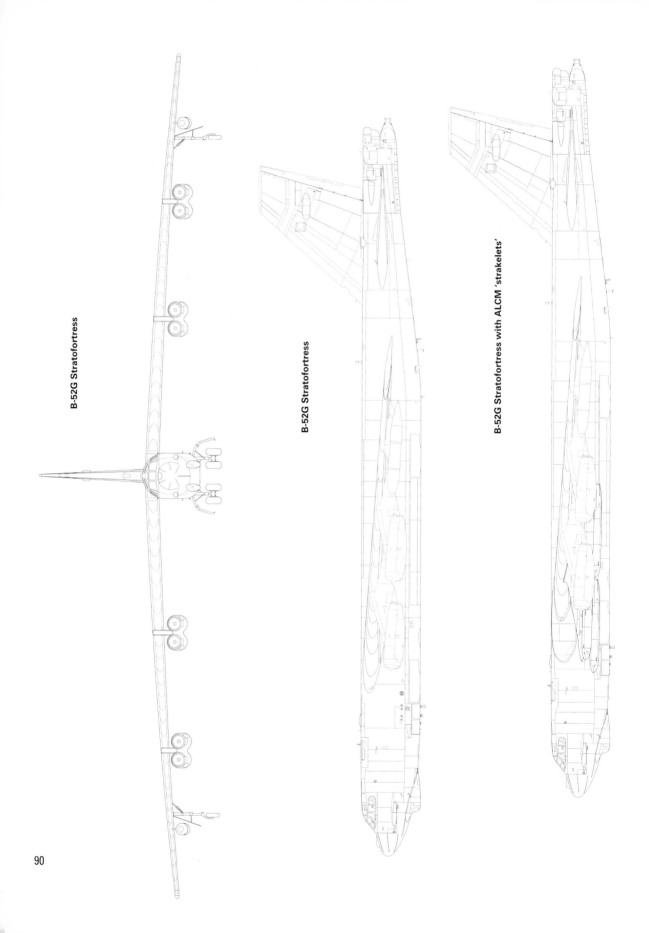

B-52G Stratofortress

B-52G Stratofortress

B-52G Stratofortress with ALCM 'strakelets'

COLOUR PLATES

1
B-52G 58-0183 *Valkyrie*, 2nd BW, Barksdale AFB, Louisiana, January 1991

When it took part in Operation *Secret Squirrel*, 58-0183 wore the Strategic Camouflage Scheme, with the 2nd BW's *Fleur de Lys* badge on the tail fin. The so-called B-52 Strategic Camouflage Scheme was the most common 'Buff' colour scheme at the time of *Desert Storm*, although both the 42nd and 93rd BWs had largely transitioned to an overall grey colour scheme. The Strategic scheme consisted of a two-tone IR dark green (FS 34086) and Euro 1 gray (FS 36081) camouflage over the upper surfaces and sides of the aircraft, with the topside grey being augmented by Gunship Quality Gray (FS 36118) on the undersides. In different lighting conditions, the upper surface colours could appear to blend together, although when well-weathered, the green could take on a reddish brown tint. *Valkyrie* was the sixth aircraft on *Secret Squirrel* – the cruise missile mission which opened Desert Storm. It was flown by Crew S-92, commanded by Captain Alan W Moe, with co-pilot Capt David T Greer Jr, radar navigator Capt Blaise M Martinick, navigator 1Lt John S Pyles, electronic warfare officer Capt Anthony Bothwell and gunner Sgt Danny L Parker. The augmentee pilots were Capt Joseph M Hasbrouck and Maj Steven D Weilbrenner (this aircraft was the only one to carry two augmentee pilots), and Capt Matthew G Caselle was the augmentee navigator. *Valkyrie* escaped the AMARC guillotine, and is today on display in the Pima County Air Museum, which is located on the perimeter of Davis-Monthan AFB.

2
B-52G 58-0185 *El Lobo II*, 2nd BW, Barksdale AFB, Louisiana, January 1991

The white nose of B-52s painted in the original SAC camouflage scheme (sometimes known as the SIOP scheme) proved extremely visible, especially at low level, and many aircraft had their radomes simply overpainted in Gray FS 36081. The rest of the aircraft remained in tan (FS 34201), green (FS 34159) and dark green (FS 34079) camouflage, with white undersides. *El Lobo II* was one of the few B-52s still wearing the old colour scheme when *Desert Storm* began, and it may have been the only participating aircraft that was so decorated. The bomber was the seventh, and final, aircraft on the *Secret Squirrel* mission, flying as 'Doom 37'. It was flown by Crew S-93, under the command of Capt Stephen D Sicking, with co-pilot 1Lt Russell F Mathers, radar navigator Capt Floyd W Gowans, navigator 1Lt Gregory D Moss, electronic warfare officer Capt Paul M Benson and gunner S/Sgt William J LeClair. Augmentee aircrew were Capt Steven W Kirkpatrick (augmentee pilot) and Maj Fredrick D Van Wicklin (augmentee navigator). *El Lobo II* resides at the Air Force Armament Museum at Eglin AFB, Florida.

3
B-52G 59-2582 *Grim Reaper II*, 2nd BW, Barksdale AFB, Louisiana, January 1991

Grim Reaper II was the third *Secret Squirrel* B-52G despatched by the 2nd BW on the historic mission. The aircraft wore the first B-52 grey colour scheme (known officially as the Monochromatic Camouflage Scheme), using Gray FS 36081 overall. This was the shade of grey used on the upper surfaces of KC-10 Extenders and KC-135 Stratotankers, and was darker than the gunship grey used later. The aircraft was flown by Capt Charles E Jones Jr, with co-pilot Capt Warren G Ward, radar navigator Capt Patrick Hobday, navigator 1Lt Aaron E Hattabaugh, electronic warfare officer Capt Kevin M Williams and gunner Sgt William J McCutchen. The aircraft also carried augmentee pilot Maj William H Weller and augmentee navigator Maj Bruce F Blood.

4
B-52G 57-6472 *MAD DOG*, 801st BW(P), Moron AB, Spain, January 1991

One of eight 801st BW(P) B-52Gs drawn from Wurtsmith's 379th BW, *MAD DOG* wore the latter wing's distinctive 'Triangle K' tail marking. It flew 11 *Desert Storm* missions, totalling 173.9 flying hours. Like all of the 379th aircraft used in the campaign, 57-6472 wore strategic camouflage. The combat veteran arrived at AMARC on 8 July 1992.

5
B-52G 57-6508 *OUT HOUSE MOUSE II*, 801st BW(P), Moron AB, Spain, January 1991

57-6508 was one of seven 2nd BW B-52Gs which flew missions from Moron during *Desert Storm*. The aircraft wore strategic camouflage and carried the wing's distinctive *Fleur de Lys* insignia on its tail fin. *OUT HOUSE MOUSE II* flew only five missions during the campaign, all from Moron, totalling 79.2 flying hours. During the late 1980s, Barksdale's B-52Gs were painted with World War 2- era Eighth Air Force nose art. Crew chiefs were able to choose the nose art from a designated book, so the personal markings adorning these aircraft in *Desert Storm* echoed art that had previously appeared on wartime Eighth Air Force B-17s. This connection reflected the fact that the Eighth Air Force HQ was located at Barksdale. *OUT HOUSE MOUSE II* ended its 15,510 flying-hour career on 22 July 1992 when it flew to AMARC. The B-52 was eliminated on 28 September 2000.

6
B-52G 57-6515 *Mohawk Warrior*, 801st BW(P), Moron AB, Spain, February 1991

91

Mohawk Warrior was painted in the most recent, lighter overall grey colour scheme. This used the same Gray FS 366118 ('Gunship Gray') as was employed as the base colour for the C-141 and C-5 camouflage scheme, as well as the AC-130. The new shade replaced the original grey from late 1990. Drawn from the 416th BW at Griffiss, *Mohawk Warrior's* Statue of Liberty tail markings were very neatly painted over so that virtually no trace remained. The bomber returned to Griffiss after flying four operational missions, totalling 64.9 hours. It was sent to AMARC on 30 September 1992, with 14,121 hours 'on the clock'. The B-52 was eliminated on 30 March 2001.

7

B-52G 58-0170 *Special Delivery II*, 801st BW(P), Moron AB, Spain, February 1991
Special Delivery II wore the Statue of Liberty tail markings of the 416th BW from Griffiss AFB, New York. Camouflaged in monochromatic grey overall, the aircraft ended the war with a bomb-log showing 20 black bombs (the first three with a red strike-through, symbolising recalls), although it actually flew 23 missions, and had one further recall. One of nine 416th BW B-52Gs operated from Moron during the war, 58-0170 had 337.8 combat hours to its credit, and was the fourth 'hardest used' B-52 assigned to the 801st. The bomber flew exclusively from Moron during the war. 58-0170 made its final flight (to AMARC) on 10 November 1992, concluding 13,521 flying hours. It was eliminated on 17 March 1998.

8

B-52G 58-0245 *EQUIPOISE II*, 806th BW(P), RAF Fairford, United Kingdom, March 1991
The 2nd BW's 58-0245 flew two missions from Moron (totalling 29 hours) before transferring to Fairford, where the aircraft completed nine more missions (plus an abort and a diversion to Jeddah, adding a further 133 hours). It ended the war with a bomb-log consisting of nine diagonal red bombs and a small Iraqi flag. Named *EQUIPOISE II*, the aircraft's nose art took the form of a small and discreet Pegasus. It was retired to AMARC on 20 October 1992 and was eliminated on 28 June 2001, having amassed 13,860 flying hours.

9

B-52G 57-6498 *ACE IN THE HOLE*, 806th BW(P), RAF Fairford, United Kingdom, March 1991
57-6498 (a former ALCM test aircraft) gained its *ACE IN THE HOLE* nickname and nose art before the war, when still painted in three-tone strategic camouflage. The artwork and titling was carefully masked out when the aircraft was repainted in the original darker grey colour scheme. However, the distinctive Statue of Liberty tail markings of the 416th BW were hastily, and crudely, overpainted in fresher, darker, glossier grey paint. By the time the war finished, 57-6498 had a bomb-log consisting of ten diagonal red bomb silhouettes and a single small Iraqi flag, although USAF records suggest

that the B-52 actually amassed its 177.1 combat flying hours in 11 missions from Fairford. By the time *ACE IN THE HOLE* was retired to AMARC on 3 November 1992, it was wearing the badge of the 2nd BW, but the bomber had retained its wartime nose art and bomb-log. The jet was eliminated on 19 July 1995, having flown 17,143 hours.

10

B-52G 58-0168 *Treasure Hunter*, 801st BW(P), Moron AB, Spain, January 1991
Wearing a coonskin cap, and with a camera around his neck and a musket and a bomb in either hand, the *Treasure Hunter* on the nose of the 379th BW's 58-0168 was recognisably based on the Warner Brothers' cartoon cat, Sylvester. He brought enough luck to his crews that the aircraft flew two missions from Fairford and nine from Moron, amassing 175.9 combat flying hours. The aircraft's 'Triangle K' tail markings were eventually overpainted. Barely had *Treasure Hunter* returned to CONUS when it was despatched to AMARC on 22 October 1991.

11

B-52G 58-0182 *What's Up DOC?*, 806th BW(P), RAF Fairford, United Kingdom, February 1991
Like many of its 379th BW wing-mates, 58-0182 carried nose art based on a Warner Brothers cartoon figure, in this case Bugs Bunny. Reclining on a stylised bomber, this winking Bugs brandished a carrot in his right hand, with a bomb held in his feet. *What's Up DOC?* flew eight missions from Fairford, totalling 105.5 hours, and one 16.1-hour mission from Moron. The aircraft's Fairford missions were marked with a line of diagonal red bombs, while the Moron groundcrew applied a single, subtle, black bomb. The aircraft retained its peacetime 'Triangle K' tail markings throughout the war. Flown to AMARC on 10 June 1992, 58-0182 was eliminated on 9 April 1996, having completed 8768 flying hours.

12

B-52G 58-0204 *Special Delivery*, 806th BW(P), RAF Fairford, United Kingdom, February 1991
When 58-0204 (the former *Rivet Ace* testbed) arrived at Fairford, it wore the distinctive 'Triangle K' tail marking of the 379th BMW, but the bomber's nose art was soon overpainted in dull red. The artwork had featured a liveried waiter carrying a tray on which rested six fused bombs. A label streamed from one of these, bearing the words *Special Delivery*, and this escaped the attentions of the censors. 58-0204 flew six missions with the 806th BW(P), totalling 86.5 flying hours, as well as two aborts and one diversion to Jeddah. 58-0204 was retired to AMARC on 24 September 1991.

13

B-52G 58-0231 *High Roller*, 806th BW(P), RAF Fairford, United Kingdom, February 1991
The 416th BW's 58-0231 lost its 'Lady Liberty' tail

emblem during *Desert Storm*, although this was so neatly overpainted in dark grey and black as to leave what was, in effect, a 'toned down' 'lo-vis' version of the marking! The aircraft's *High Roller* nose art was also obliterated, although not with the same level of care as the tail markings. The aircraft ended the war with 61.5 combat flying hours and four missions to its credit. The bomber arrived at AMARC on 3 December 1992.

14
B-52G 58-0247 *High Plains Drifter*, 806th BW(P), RAF Fairford, United Kingdom, February 1991
58-0247 lost its *High Plains Drifter* nose art during *Desert Storm*, but retained full 379th BW 'Triangle K' tail markings. The nose art consisted of a mounted cowboy hurling a yellow bomb over his arm. Like *High Roller*, this was obliterated with the application of a patch of red-brown paint, The aircraft flew three sorties from Fairford, totalling 51.9 combat flying hours. The *High Plains Drifter* was retired to AMARC on 5 November 1991.

15
B-52G 58-0212, 1500th SW(P), Andersen AFB, Guam, January 1991
The 1500th SW(P) was formed at Andersen AFB from aircraft and crews drawn from the 42nd and 93rd BWs, pending the availability of bases in Saudi Arabia. 58-0212, from the 93rd BW, was flown on to the 4300th BW(P) on the first day of the war by a crew which included navigator Jim Clonts. The aircraft completed 17 missions from Diego Garcia, totalling 262.9 flying hours. 58-0212 was one of the last B-52Gs in service, being finally retired to AMARC on 8 February 1994.

16
B-52G 57-6492 *Old Crow Express*, 1708th BW(P), King Abdul Aziz IAP, Jeddah (Jeddah New), Saudi Arabia, March 1991
Old Crow Express of the 379th BW was the fifth 'hardest worked' B-52G of the 1708th BW(P), amassing 233.1 flying hours during the course of 54 missions – it ended the war with 54 bomb symbols on its nose, all bar one (the 50th) of which were applied in white. This aircraft was one of those which began its war with a long range, 16.1-hour, mission to Iraq from its base at Wurtsmith, flying as the third B-52 in Cell 2, with Capt Steve Heflin at the controls. Only the four B-52s in Cell 2 actually dropped bombs on Iraq. Cell 1 was recalled by an E-3 Sentry AWACS aircraft before it could drop its ordnance, while Cell 3 ran low on fuel after being forced to bypass a storm en route to the target. Wurtsmith's final B-52G, 57-6492 departed for AMARC on 15 December 1992, piloted by 379th BW CO, Col William H Campbell Jr. The aircraft was eliminated on 30 July 2001.

17
B-52G 57-6509 *NINE O NINE II*, 1708th BW(P), King Abdul Aziz IAP, Jeddah (Jeddah New), Saudi Arabia, March 1991

Although the 1708th BW(P) drew most of its assets from the 42nd, 379th, 93rd and 416th BWs, *NINE O NINE II* came from Barksdale's 2nd BW, having flown three missions (totalling 40.5 flying hours) with the 801st BW(P) at Moron. At Jeddah, 57-6509 flew 29 missions (134.5 flying hours). Interestingly, the aircraft's bomb-log showed 30 white bomb symbols (indicating missions from Jeddah) and four black (missions from Moron), plus a camel and a palm tree. The aircraft was eventually delivered to the Eighth Air Force Museum at Barksdale on 16 September 1992, having amassed 14,515 flying hours.

18
B-52G 58-0164 *SAC TIME*, 1708th BW(P), King Abdul Aziz IAP, Jeddah (Jeddah New), Saudi Arabia, March 1991
The 416th BW's 58-0164 wore a Vargas girl-style nose art, together with the name *SAC TIME*. Featuring Statue of Liberty tail markings, the aircraft flew six missions (although its bomb-log showed seven black bombs), totalling 77.8 flying hours, from Moron. The bomber then transferred to Jeddah, where it flew 26 more sorties, totalling 119.3 hours. The aircraft was retired to AMARC on 5 November 1992.

19
B-52G 58-0173 *LET'S MAKE A DEAL*, 1708th BW(P), King Abdul Aziz IAP, Jeddah (Jeddah New), Saudi Arabia, March 1991
Standing atop a cloud, shaking his left fist and getting ready to throw a fizzing bomb, the Donald Duck on the nose of 58-0173 did not look ready to 'make a deal'! This aircraft was the lead jet in the first cell of B-52s which deployed to Jeddah on an operational mission launched from Wurtsmith at the start of the war. On this 18.5-hour mission, the aircraft was flown by Crew S-30, captained by Capt Reed Estrada, and including Capt Andy Bloom, who provided many of the photographs in this book. *LET'S MAKE A DEAL* was drawn from the 379th BW, and wore the wing's distinctive 'Triangle K' tail markings. It flew 42 missions from Jeddah, totalling 190.6 flying hours. The aircraft retired to AMARC on 5 August 1992, and was eliminated on 19 July 1995 with 14,331 flying hours 'on the clock'.

20
B-52G 58-0175 *VIPER*, 1708th BW(P), King Abdul Aziz IAP, Jeddah (Jeddah New), Saudi Arabia, January 1991
Capt Seth Junkins and Crew S-10 flew 58-0175 on its first 17.4-hour mission of the war, taking off from Wurtsmith to bomb Iraq and land back at Jeddah as the lead aircraft in the third cell. Like other 379th BW B-52Gs, *VIPER* wore strategic camouflage and the prominent 'Triangle K' tail marking. The aircraft flew 47 missions from Jeddah, amassing 215.8 combat flying hours. *VIPER* was subsequently retired to AMARC on 16 October 1991.

VIPER was subsequently retired to AMARC on 16 October 1991.

21
B-52G 58-0194 *BUFFASAURUS*, 1708th BW(P), King Abdul Aziz IAP, Jeddah (Jeddah New), Saudi Arabia, March 1991

The BUFFASAURUS nose art applied to 58-0194 summed up the 379th BW's Cold War role – using an 'aeronautical dinosaur' to deliver cruise missiles. Wearing the usual 379th BW colour scheme of strategic camouflage, with 'Triangle K' tail markings, BUFFASAURUS deployed to Jeddah as the lead aircraft in the second cell, bombing targets in Iraq after taking off from Wurtsmith. The aircraft was flown on this 15.8-hour mission by Crew S-20, captained by Capt Berry Sebring. The aircraft flew 46 further missions from Jeddah (208.2 hours). While being flown by one Capt Batway, BUFFASAURUS was heavily damaged by a SAM, losing its left outboard fuel tank. 58-0194 retired to AMARC on 23 October 1991, and was eliminated ten years later on 30 April 2001, having flown 12,942 flying hours.

22
B-52G 58-0195 *ETERNAL GUARDIAN*, 1708th BW(P), King Abdul Aziz IAP, Jeddah (Jeddah New), Saudi Arabia, March 1991

58-0195 was the only B-52G to fly operational missions with three of the four provisional wings formed for Desert Storm. Undertaking long distance sorties from Moron (two, totalling 32.5 hours) and Diego Garcia (one 10.7-hour hop), the aircraft also completed 46 missions from Jeddah (totalling 194.1 hours). These sorties combined made it the eighth top-scoring aircraft mission wise. Known as ETERNAL GUARDIAN pre- and post-war, the aircraft did not carry nose art during Desert Storm. Like a number of the 42nd BW jets involved in the conflict, 58-0195 wore the Strategic Camouflage Scheme, with the wing's moose head insignia in toned-down form, the name LORING down the tailplane and the legend THE MOOSE IS LOOSE over the crew data panel. ETERNAL GUARDIAN was eliminated on 18 November 1993, with 13,947 flying hours on the clock.

23
B-52G 58-0253 *APPETITE FOR DESTRUCTION*, 1708th BW(P), King Abdul Aziz IAP, Jeddah (Jeddah New), Saudi Arabia, March 1991

58-0253 wore the name APPETITE FOR DESTRUCTION on the crew panel, below the usual 42nd BW THE MOOSE IS LOOSE legend. The name Pamela III was applied between the two, in dark grey. The aircraft flew one 11.1-hour mission from Diego Garcia before transferring to Jeddah on 17 January 1991. As part of the 1708th BW(P) the B-52 accumulated a further 214.6 combat flying hours in 52 sorties. The aircraft was retired to AMARC on 4 November 1993.

24
B-52G 57-6473 *Hard t'get*, 4300th BW(P), Diego Garcia, British Indian Ocean Territory, January 1991

All of the B-52Gs assigned to the 4300th BW(P) at Diego Garcia came from the 42nd and 93rd BWs, and most were painted in the dark grey colour scheme. 57-6473 Hard t'get is often described as being from the 2nd BW, but when assigned to Diego Garcia, it actually belonged to the 93rd BW (the Stratofortress training wing) at Castle AFB. As such, the aircraft wore the 93rd's stylised 'rook' (chess piece) badge, rather than the Fleur de Lys of the 2nd BW. 57-6473 flew 18 missions, totalling 249.9 combat flying hours. On 25 February 1993 57-6473 was finally retired to AMARC.

25
B-52G 58-0202, 4300th BW(P), Diego Garcia, British Indian Ocean Territory, March 1991

Apart from the usual 42nd BW THE MOOSE IS LOOSE motto, 58-0202 went to war without a name or nose art. The aircraft did wear the 42nd BW's moose head tail markings, however. The aircraft flew 18 missions from Diego Garcia, totalling 278.7 combat flying hours. The first bomb on its mission log was applied by navigator Jim Clonts, who kindly assisted in the preparation of this book. 58-0202 was among the last B-52Gs in service, finally flying to AMARC on 10 March 1994.

26
B-52G 58-0233, 4300th BW(P), Diego Garcia, British Indian Ocean Territory, January 1991

The 42nd and 93rd BWs' B-52Gs were extremely anonymous, most of them painted in the monochromatic grey colour scheme, and without names or nose art. 58-0233 of the 93rd BW was typical, its drab finish being lifted only by the Castle tail badge, a small wing badge on the port forward fuselage and SAC's crest to starboard. The aircraft flew 18 Desert Storm missions, logging 241.9 hours in the process. 58-0233 reached AMARC on 17 February 1994.

27
B-52G 58-0248 *IN HARM'S WAY*, 4300th BW(P), Diego Garcia, British Indian Ocean Territory, February 1991

58-0248 flew only a single 4.5-hour mission before being badly damaged, officially by an enemy SAM. The aircraft had the aft six to eight feet of its rear fuselage blown off, severing the rear gun turret and ECM jammers. During a programme shown on the Discovery Wings channel, the aircrew recounted that they were in a very high angle bank when they were hit by ground fire. Others suggest that the gunner had turned his defensive fire control systems radar on at exactly the wrong moment, just as a nearby F-4G 'Wild Weasel' fired an AGM-88 HARM at a ground threat. The missile homed onto the DFCS radar emissions. The aircraft took no further part in the war, instead being ferried to Guam, where a team of volunteers repaired the jet using the rear fuselage of an aircraft grounded at Andersen AFB by an irreparable wing spar crack. Rectification work took seven weeks to complete, after which the aircraft flew home to Castle with a fully working gun and defensive systems. It was retired to AMARC on 25 January 1994.

Back cover
B-52G 58-0159 *Alley Oops Bold Assault*, 1708th BW(P), King Abdul Aziz IAP, Jeddah (Jeddah

New), Saudi Arabia, January 1991
The nose art adorning Alley Oops Bold Assault featured an angry, club-wielding caveman about to hurl a bomb. Many felt that the prehistoric theme was entirely appropriate for such an old aircraft. 58-0159 was the second B-52 in the third wave of aircraft which took off from Wurtsmith to bomb Iraq, before landing at their deployed base at Jeddah. It was flown on this 17.5-hour mission by Capt Bill Borras, with Crew R-15. Jeddah did not remove the 'Triangle K' tail markings used by the

BIBLIOGRAPHY

Boeing B-52 Stratofortress by Peter E Davies and Tony Thornborough, Crowood, 1998

B-52 Stratofortress – Boeing's Cold War Warrior by R F Dorr and L Peacock, Osprey, 1995

Boeing B-52 A Documentary History by Walter Boyne, Jane's, 1981

B-52 Stratofortress by Jeff Ethell and Joe Christy, Ian Allan, 1981

B-52 Ageing BUFFs Youthful Crews by René J Francillon and Peter B Lewis, Osprey, 1988

B-52 Stratofortress in Action by Larry Davis, Squadron/Signal, 1992

Boeing B-52G/H Stratofortress – Aerofax Datagraph 7 by Dennis R Jenkins and Brian Rogers, Aerofax, 1990

B-52 Stratofortress in Detail and Scale by Alwyn T Lloyd, Detail and Scale, 1988

B-52 – Aeroguide 28 by Anthony Thornborough, Linewrights, 1990

B-52, Przeglad Konstrukcii Lotniczych, 1992

Walk Around B-52 Stratofortress by Lou Drendel, Squadron/Signal, 1996

ACC Bomber Triad by Don Logan, Schiffer, 1999

Air Power in the Gulf by James P Coyne, Aerospace Education Foundation, 1992

Air Power The Coalition and Iraqi Air Forces by Roy Braybrook, Osprey, 1991

Air War Desert Storm by Lou Drendel, Squadron/Signal, 1991

Allied Aircraft Art by John M and Donna Campbell, Schiffer, 1992

Assessing the Victory Persian Gulf War by Aviation Week and Space Technology, 1991

Birds of Prey by David F Brown, Schiffer, 1993

Desert Storm Air War by Robert F Dorr, Motorbooks, 1991

The Fury of Desert Storm – the Air Campaign by Bert Kinzey, TAB, 1991

Gulf Air War Debrief by Stan Morse, Aerospace, 1991

Painted Ladies Modern Military Aircraft Nose Art and Unusual Markings by Randy Walker, Schiffer, 1992

Planes, Names and Dames, Vol III 1955–1975, by Larry Davis, Squadron/Signal, 1995

Shark's Teeth Nose Art by Jeffrey L Ethell, Motorbooks, 1992

Strategic Air Command by Lindsay T Peacock, 1988

Strategic Air Command Unit Mission and History Summaries, HQ SAC, 1988,

Superbase Barksdale by David Davies and Mike Vines, Osprey, 1991

US Aircraft and Armament of Operation Desert Storm by Bert Kinzey, Detail and Scale, 1993

US Airpower in Desert Storm by Michael Green, Concord, 1991

USAF Strike Aircraft by Joe Cupido, Osprey, 1991

USAF Colours and Markings in the 1990s by Dana Bell, Greenhill, 1992

Operation Desert Storm: Evaluation of the Air Campaign (Letter Report, 06/12/97, GAO/NSIAD-97-134)

Limits on the Role and Performance of B-52 Bombers in Conventional Conflicts (GAO/NSIAD-93-138, May 12, 1993)

INDEX

References to illustrations are shown in **bold**.Colour plate illustrations are prefixed 'cp.', with page and caption locators in brackets.